The emphasis in this book upon hearing God in the Bible is a most needed one. The centrality of Scripture to Christian understanding and spiritual growth is often affirmed but not always practiced in a meaningful way. This volume by Keith Shearer can help. The author carefully shows the difference between just affirming a creed and actually understanding what the Bible is saying. The admonition to interpret the Bible "as it reads" will guard the reader from narrowness or misdirected zeal. I heartily recommend its emphasis and practical suggestions.

                        Homer A. Kent, President Emeritus
                        Grace College and Seminary
                        Winona Lake, Indiana

In this eloquent and moving presentation of recovering our Bibles from the trap of neglect, Dr. Shearer challenges us in the Grace Brethren movement to reclaim the Bible as our central authority. In his distinctive voice he opens us up to rediscover the essential truth of God's Word in our life. Such truth drives us not only to serve our Savior out of the flow of our rich heritage, but with the true joy that only comes from faith in Christ and His Word! You will be nourished and touched by the wisdom of this work!

                        Tim Boal, Executive Director
                        Grace Brethren North American Missions

Satan's first temptation aimed to cause Eve to doubt God's Word. Paul warns that in the last days men will reject God's Word and will turn their hearts to fables. The Scriptures claim to speak God's Word; apart from them, we are left to speculation and vain imaginations. I applaud your desire to rekindle a passion for knowing God through His Scriptures and by His Spirit. Such passion must give God pleasure and will restore confidence to His people.

            Pastor Jim Custer
            Grace Brethren Church, Columbus, Ohio

What a needed emphasis! Thanks to the excellence of Keith Shearer's insights, this book reminds the reader why the Bible must remain our focus of life. Keith practices what he preaches in this book. He makes the Scriptures come alive. Thanks for challenging us to reclaim our Bibles—helping us keep "the main thing, the main thing."

> Ed Lewis, Executive Director
> CE National
> Fellowship of Grace Brethren Churches

CHILDLIKE
FAITH

Hearing God in Your Bible

Keith A. Shearer

BMH Books
www.bmhbooks.com

CHILDLIKE FAITH
Hearing God in Your Bible

Copyright © 2005 by Keith A. Shearer
All rights reserved. No part of this book may be reproduced in any form without permission in writing from the publisher, except in the case of brief quotations embodied in critical articles or reviews.

ISBN 10: 0-88469-301-5
ISBN 13: 978-88469-301-7

Printed in the United States of America

Scripture quotations, unless otherwise indicated, are from the New American Standard Bible®, Copyright © 1960, 1962, 1963, 1968, 1971, 1972, 1973, 1975, 1977, 1995 by The Lockman Foundation. Used by permission. www.Lockman.org

Cover design by Terry Julien
Internal page design and typesetting by Jim Folsom

BMH Books
P.O. Box 544
Winona Lake, IN 46590
www.bmhbooks.com

Dedication

It is my honor to dedicate this book to the memory of my Father, Harold W. Shearer (1927-2001), from whom I learned to stand for the truth always, no matter what it costs.

Acknowledgments

Thanks to the staff of BMH Books for their excellent work. In 2004, BMH director Terry White observed me at a table doing research and motivated me to put the content into book form. His push started this project. Jesse Deloe, who has been a significant personal encouragement to me for many years, has again been a highly valuable source of help through his keen editing skills.

Susan Myer, my secretary, deserves many thanks for providing help with typing and computer work. I am grateful as well to my sisters and brothers in Christ at New Beginnings Grace Brethren Church for their encouragement and prayers throughout the project.

Many conversations surrounding the ideas of this book have helped form it. My appreciation goes to these friends who listened and spoke in those conversations – Dan Allan, Tom Avey, Tim Boal, Jim Custer, Dave Guiles, Dan Jackson, Tom Julien, Ed Lewis, Dan O'Deens, Tim Sheaffer, and John Teevan. Others, too numerous to list, have helped shape my thoughts also.

My unending thanks go to Laura, my wife, for her steadfastness, support, encouragement, love, devotion, and patience. Without her, my work would not be possible.

And, of course, *soli Deo Gloria*.

Keith Shearer
Myerstown, Pennsylvania
September 2005

Contents

Introduction 1
    Chapter 1: Coming to the Book 5

Section One — Biblical Authority 13
    Chapter 2: Bowing Before the God of the Book 15
    Chapter 3: The Book in Your Hands 19
    Chapter 4: The Book as It Reads 23

Section Two — Childlike Faith 27
    Chapter 5: Childlike Faith 29
    Chapter 6: Understanding with Your Heart 33

Section Three — Submissive Obedience 37
    Chapter 7: The Obedience of Childlike Faith 39
    Chapter 8: To Change Your Life 43
    Chapter 9: This Book Will Keep You from Sin 45
    Chapter 10: Immediacy 49

Section Four — Communal Interpretation 53
    Chapter 11: The Church—Understanding in Community 55
    Chapter 12: Hearing—Word, Spirit, and Community 61
    Chapter 13: No Other Creed 69

Section Five — Transformational Separation 75
    Chapter 14: Not Conformed to this World 77
    Chapter 15: Separation Without Isolation 81

Section Six — Missionary Dynamic 87
    Chapter 16: Reading Like a Missionary 89

Section Seven — Sufficient Grace 95
    Chapter 17: The Promise of the Future 97
    Chapter 18: Every Promise in the Book Is Mine 103
    Chapter 19: Reading Someone Else's Mail 107

Endnotes 113

Foreword

He who has ears to hear, let him hear.

This statement of our Lord is found immediately after his parable of the four soils, representing four different responses to the Word of God. The implication is clear: it is one thing to have ears; it is another to hear.

In *Childlike Faith*, Keith Shearer applies this truth to today's reader of God's Word. Most people reading the Bible have no problem believing that it is God's message. How many, however, really hear what God is saying?

The message of this book is sorely needed in our times. It is not enough merely to read the Bible; we must hear what it is saying. What we hear will be determined by many factors, including our beliefs, our attitudes, our behavior patterns, the influence of other Christians, our vision of what God is doing in the world, and the influence of God's Spirit on our hearts.

This book is a panorama of these factors. In his book Dr. Shearer treats such things as Biblical authority, obedience, the weight of the community, separation, mission and grace—all of these having significant influence on our understanding of the Word of God.

It is a book that will require reflection, but reflection that will pay high dividends.

> Tom Julien, Missionary Statesman
> Former Executive Director,
> Grace Brethren International Missions
> Winona Lake, Indiana

Introduction

I love the Bible because I love the God of the Bible. The Bible is His very Word. Since it is His Word, I treasure every word of it, for every word is a word from my Creator—Sustainer—Redeemer—Savior—Lover—King. If I do not value the Bible in this way, I raise the question as to whether or not I actually believe the Bible is the Word of God.

It is possible to believe that the Bible is the Word of God as a proposition, and even to affirm its inspiration, inerrancy, and infallibility as the essential planks in one's theological platform, but still not love and treasure it. It is even possible to spend thousands of hours in diligent, rigorous, disciplined, academic study of the Bible, yet still be extraordinarily shallow and lifeless in one's knowledge and love of God.

This book is to help us approach our Bibles with the joy of the psalmist who exclaimed, "I shall delight in Your commandments, which I love; and I shall lift up my hands to Your commandments, which I love; and I will meditate on Your statutes" (Psalm 119:47-48). A reading of Psalm 119 will give a sense of what this book is attempting to accomplish.

I want to help us reclaim our Bibles. Yes, physically they have not yet been taken from us as they have been from others both past and present. But, can we lose the joyful desire for our Bibles, and does that loss have the same effect as having our Bibles stolen from us? Our Bibles can become lost in the overwhelming mass of emotional and time demands, so that we lack energy and "just don't feel like it" when it comes to reading the Bible.

The Bible can be held hostage by specific cultural and political persuasions designed to accomplish an agenda so perplexing and frustrating that we wonder if God really can speak His own Word to our culture. The Bible can be stolen from us even in church, at college, at seminary, in a bookstore, over the radio or by other media—and not necessarily from bad or false teaching. The volume of well-intentioned teaching can produce debilitating exhaustion and disagreements (whether real or perceived) over methods, translations, interpretations, or denominations.

So we hear, "I can't possibly understand the Bible. If the experts can't agree on what it means, who am I to interpret it?" Or, "The Bible is just not enjoyable anymore, because for every insight I get from it, there is a preacher or scholar somewhere telling me I'm wrong." And there are dozens of similar responses.

I am not advocating that we diminish or dismiss any biblical doctrine. We are, with the Apostle Paul, "appointed for the defense of the gospel" (Philippians 1:16). We believe and keep these biblical truths, not from pharisaical layers of cultural, theological, methodological, or political impositions upon the Bible.

Again, I am not ignoring the role of history and the community of the church in understanding Scripture—in fact I am promoting them. We do need more and constantly

Introduction

improved teaching, whether in churches, schools, books, or radio programs. But we need them to lift and draw us back into our enjoyment of God and His Word.

This book is to help us feel free and thrilled about receiving insights from God in His Word. Ours could be an experience like that of Hilkiah (2 Kings 22:8), who "found the book of the law in the house of the Lord," rediscovering the Bible where it was meant to be heard and loved the whole time.

Believers in Jesus Christ who have had Bibles denied to them have often been able to endure persecution and martyrdom with faith and spiritual courage because they have had a deposit of the Bible already stored and valued inside themselves. This deposit is the tool and the treasure of the Holy Spirit, which no one can take from them. Such is the universal testimony. How is it for us, and how will it be for us in times of hardship?

There is another purpose for this book. I have discovered that the way I read the Bible is also the way a group of believers called "Grace Brethren" read the Bible. Historic movements and discipleship trends have influenced people's values and attitudes in the way they approach the Bible. I find it interesting and compelling that the values formed in the Grace Brethren movement are unique, attractive, helpful, positive, and beautiful. In fact, when I began this project, I first called it "Mack, McClain, and the Bible."

If you are a Grace Brethren reader, I hope this book makes you rejoice in our core identity as Bible-people. If you are not Grace Brethren, I hope the approach described here is, or becomes, yours.

Now, Lord, "Open my eyes, that I may behold wonderful things from Your law" (Psalm 119:18).

CHAPTER **ONE**

COMING TO THE BOOK

Most fundamentally, their careful reading of the New Testament taught them that the Apostolic Church required its followers (1) to manifest a devout, childlike faith; (2) to be of one mind in matters of faith and practice; (3) to deny their own selfish wills and submit to the laws of God's household; and (4) to separate themselves from the sinful nature of the world around them. These element—childlike faith, unity, obedience, and separation—constituted the heart of the Brethren faith. – Carl F. Bowman[1]

Then here is another lesson: the Jews studied their Scriptures, and yet they utterly failed to see the truth. There is a possibility of that today. It is possible for a man to study diligently the Word of God, but if he does not see Jesus, it will profit him nothing. – Alva J. McClain[2]

Our approach to the Bible is crucial. What is our intent when we come to the Book? What are our desires and attitudes? How we answer these questions colors everything we see or do not see in the Bible.

Our view of the Bible is influenced by multiple factors—upbringing, cultural environment, church experience, language, education, relationships, and more. But the strongest influence is the sovereign working of the Triune God. Within each of us who are trusting in Jesus Christ alone for our salvation, God the Holy Spirit has created and is creating a love and desire for His Word. In groups and movements of God's people, the Holy Spirit brings seasons of refinement, or change points, to guide us providentially in our understanding of His Word. We do not really read the Bible alone. We are always influenced. How we approach the Bible is a question about who and what has influenced us, how they have influenced us, and whether or not theirs has been a good influence.

The reading of Church history from the apostolic era to their own time was a starting point of influence in the Bible reading of the early Brethren. What they saw was an ideal of the primitive church, the church of the New Testament. Therefore, "the primary impulse of the early Brethren was to restore" the church to the ideal New Testament condition, or in their words, "earnestly contending for the faith once delivered to the saints."[3]

Alexander Mack (1679-1735) of the first Brethren fellowship at Schwarzenau, Germany, stressed, "We indeed have neither a new church nor any new laws. We only want to remain in simplicity and true faith in the original church which Jesus founded through His blood. We wish to obey the commandment which was in the beginning."[4]

This concept of the primitive church, though capable of being abused, has motivated the Grace Brethren movement always to return to the primitive text, the Bible itself, as the only rule and authority of faith and practice. Creeds and confessions have been rejected as additions to or subtractions from the Gospel.[5] The concept also has encouraged Grace Brethren to value the reading and study of the biblical text in its original languages, so that their understanding might be as close to the original intent as possible and then lived out in contemporary settings.

To amplify on Carl F. Bowman's excellent analysis, the Brethren clearly saw from their study of the New Testament that the early church practiced (1) a sincere, childlike faith (Matthew 18:3-6; 1 Peter 2:2); (2) a denial of their own selfish wills and submission to God's will (Luke 9:23-25; 22:42); (3) community of love and single-mindedness in faith and practice (John 13:34-35; Acts 1:14; Philippians 2:1-5); and (4) separation from sinful worldliness with transformation into Christ likeness (Romans 12:1-2; 2 Corinthians 6:14-18).

These four elements—childlike faith, obedience, community, and transformation—constituted the heart of the Brethren faith.[6] Everything else—including the practice of church discipline, believers' water baptism by triune immersion, footwashing, the love feast, anointing, and the holy kiss—flowed from this heart of childlike faith to understand and obey the mind of Christ even in the very smallest matters. They strove to practice these things as closely as possible to the manner they were originally given and practiced by the Master and His apostles.

Both Pietists and Anabaptists were and are influenced by the search for the primitive church. Anabaptists tended to focus more on external evidences of a person's relationship with Christ—hearing the Bible preached, outward obedience, the church, unity, purity, faithfulness, and relationships with others. Pietists tended to focus more on the internal—meditation on the Word, guidance of the Spirit, openness, growth, devotion, and love for God. Considering Jesus' commands in Matthew 22:37-40, the Pietists would lean to the "love the Lord your God" side, while the Anabaptists would lean to the "love your neighbor" side. Of course. these are generalizations.

What the Brethren were able to do was to view Pietism and Anabaptism as "mutually reinforcing currents" so that both could be held in creative tension.[7] "In sum, the Schwarzenau Brethren were molded by Radical Pietist understandings of spirituality and the Christian life, and by Anabaptist understandings of the church."[8] In this, similar to the Puritans and others, the Brethren promoted an evangelicalism which was a refueling of genuine Christianity against the backdrop of the spiritually lifeless and politicized Reformed and Lutheran churches.[9] Such is the beauty and attraction of the movement.

While the Brethren movement was a Pietist-Anabaptist movement reacting to what had become the deadness of the Reformation, it is not to be forgotten that the Brethren were heirs, or "stepchildren," of the Reformation.[10] The doctrinal emphases of the Reformers were shared by the Brethren to such a degree that there was little debate.[11] The deity and authority of Jesus Christ (*sola Christus*), the inspiration and infallibility of the Bible (*sola Scriptura*), the doctrines of grace (*sola gratia*), justification by faith alone (*sola fidei*), the power of the Holy Spirit working for God's glory (*soli Deo Gloria*)—all of these appear without question or hesitation in the Brethren movement.

These principles of the Reformed faith can be seen in statements like the following from Alexander Mack; although often Mack's absorption in the issues of his times and preoccupation with sanctification over justification makes his wording uncomfortable or confusing to us:

Coming to the Book

When we consider the external providence of God, which stands so clearly in the written teaching of Jesus Christ despite all controversy, does this not also seem a great miracle, that the Almighty God so cares for us that we have a sure guide, and that a light always appears for us in the darkness? May God be eternally praised and glorified for His goodness, grace, and mercy, which He still evidences even to this hour.[12]

Christ is the fulfillment of the law. Whoever believes in Him is justified. Faith in Christ produces obedience and submission to all of His words and commandments.[13]

No one can be a believer without the Holy Spirit, who must create belief.[14]

We do not endeavor to obtain salvation ... but alone by faith in Jesus…[15]

The first operation of grace in the soul is a true awakening from the carefree slumber in sin and separation from God, and a recognition of our poverty and revelation of divine life. Out of this arises in the soul the hunger and desire for help, sanctification, forgiveness of sins, and righteousness. Then grace shows how sanctification and forgiveness, indeed everything, can be received from Jesus alone.[16]

It was the renewal of the Reformed doctrines of grace in the teaching emphasis of Alva J. McClain (1888-1968) that marked the Grace Movement among the Brethren.[17] Historically speaking, the Grace Brethren are theologically both Reformed and Brethren—a unique and happy combination indeed.

The Brethren movement was marked from the start by a missional emphasis also. In the words of David R. Plaster:

> They felt a strong urgency to make known the message that had so gripped their own hearts. The missionary spirit that prevailed among them in those early days gives testimony that the movement was of God. Their enthusiasm spread from town to town. Steadily, new members were added to their group. The Brethren movement was born with an intense desire to reach out. Evangelism and missionary enterprise, seen at the very beginning, will express itself in many different ways over the next three centuries.[18]

Persecution motivated missionary activity in Europe and eventually forced migrations to America. Much like the early church events of Acts 8:1-4, the Spirit of God kept the Brethren on mission by means of conflict. The Brethren moved from Pennsylvania with the era of westward frontier expansion. Language barriers, internal conflicts, self-protectiveness, and legalism, however, too often kept the Brethren from carrying out their God-given missional calling. By the 1850s, the Holy Spirit was again impressing these believers with the necessity of missionary activity.[19] This progressive spirit eventually resulted in the Progressive Movement of the Brethren Church.[20] From within that movement came the Foreign Missionary Society in 1900, which is known today as Grace Brethren International Missions, serving globally.

The Grace Movement, now the Fellowship of Grace Brethren Churches, arose as the next phase of the Brethren movement, largely because of a "difference in how to view God's grace and the nature of salvation."[21] Alva J. McClain, the first president of Grace Theological Seminary, "emphasized the believer's assurance of salvation, the believer's security, the pre-millennial, personal return of Christ for His Church, and outlines on the brilliant arguments of the Apostle Paul in *The Epistle of Paul to the Romans* on law and grace."[22]

So, what does all of this history have to do with how we approach the Bible?[23] Remember, these movements are seasons of refinement, change points, and influences of the Spirit of God. The Primitive Church concept, the Reformation, Pietism, the Anabaptists, missionary zeal and persecution, the Progressive Movement, the Grace Movement—each of these was an influence of the Holy Spirit to help us embrace some biblical truth that helps us better approach God's Word. And, likely, the Spirit of God is not finished with this process. As more believers from more nations engage one another as an interpretive community (the Body of Christ), more insights will emerge which will help us see more fully. We all need to be humbly learning from one another.

Seven principles for approaching the Bible are clear from these Spirit-movements:

1. Biblical Authority (Reformation)
2. Childlike Faith (Pietists)
3. Submissive Obedience (Pietists)
4. Communal Interpretation (Anabaptists)
5. Transformational Separation (Anabaptists)
6. Missional Dynamic (Progressive)
7. Sufficient Grace (Grace).

The rest of this book is designed to help us unpack these seven principles of how to approach God's Word. I did not come to these principles from a study of history, but from the reading of the Bible itself, guided by the Holy Spirit. It is helpful and enjoyable to know that we are part of a movement among the people of God who see and approach Scripture in similar ways.

SECTION ONE
Biblical Authority

Chapter Two: ***Bowing Before the God of the Book***

Chapter Three: ***The Book in Your Hands***

Chapter Four: ***The Book as It Reads***

Chapter **Two**

BOWING BEFORE THE GOD OF THE BOOK

Even the casual Bible-reader has probably observed some of the book's basic claims about God. Just to name some of them:

> He is triune (2 Corinthians 13:14)
> He is the creator (Genesis 1:1)
> He is the sustainer (Colossians 1:16-17)
> He is sovereign (Daniel 4:35)
> He is the redeemer (Psalm 19:14)
> He is the judge (James 4:12)
> He is the highest king (1 Timothy 6:15)
> He is holy (1 Peter 1:16)
> He is all-powerful (Luke 1:37)
> He is all- knowing (Psalm 147:5)
> He is the provider (Matthew 7:11)
> He is gracious (John 1:16-17)

He is merciful (Psalm 103:8-17)
He is loving (Romans 5:8).

The same reader has probably observed that the Bible claims to be the very words of God. The claim is hard to miss because it is expressed in various ways, thousands of times. For example, consider Isaiah 1:2, "Listen; O heavens, and hear, O earth; for the Lord speaks ..." or Jeremiah 1:2, "to whom the word of the Lord came ..." Second Peter 1:20-21 informs us that, "No prophecy of Scripture is of one's own interpretation, for no prophecy was ever made by an act of human will, but men moved by the Holy Spirit spoke from God." Yes, there is the sense in which the Bible is the word of Moses, or David, or Daniel, or John, or Peter, or Paul, or any other biblical writer. But the Bible is uniquely the Word of God—His Word.

Second Timothy 3:16-17 is the classic passage concerning the inspiration of the Bible. Try to picture what is going on in these verses. "All Scripture is inspired by God" is quite naturally rendered "All Scripture is God-breathed." So picture your ear to God's mouth as He breathes a whisper to you. Could He speak other than truth? Would His word to you not be profitable? Would it not change you? Would you not be made adequate in a single breath from Him, equipped to do whatever He desires? This is what the Bible does.

So, here is the big question. If God is everything the Bible says He is and more, and if the Bible is His very word as it claims to be, then how should we approach the Bible?

Someone or something is an authority in your life—it is the way life works. In this sense, that authority in your life assumes infallibility. Are you infallible? Is your philosophy, or government, or education, or anything else infallible? Are your thoughts, words, or opinions infallible? I would dare say they are not.

Now what of the God of the Bible? Is He infallible? Are His thoughts and words infallible? We answer Scripturally, saying, "Yes! Yes! Infinitely yes!" This is so much a "yes" that His words are called decrees, precepts, judgments, and laws.

There are four possible approaches to the Bible. The first is "Me Without God." This approach would render God and His Word irrelevant, and make you or someone/something else of your choosing the authority in your life.

The second approach is "Me Over God." This approach definitely makes you your own authority. God and the Bible are in your thinking only to the extent that you can use them, control them, or manipulate them to your own ends. Of course, this is the way all religionists use religions of every kind.

The third possible approach is "Me Equal To God." In this approach, the Bible and the God of the Bible are only one option among many. To believe that there is only one Word of God and only one way to Him seems too narrow to those of this response. A vast array of concepts, writings, institutions, or people (including oneself) can all be considered to be in authority. The Bible becomes an anthology of sayings and stories that the reader draws from when it is deemed helpful. To imagine the Bible to be fully and solely authoritative probably seems outlandish to holders of this view. In time of crisis, this way brings only confusion, deception, and fear.

The final approach is "God Over Me" in which the Triune God of the Bible is your infallible authority, and the Bible alone is His Word. This is the view that understands

CHILDLIKE **FAITH**

that if God is everything the Bible says He is and more, and if the Bible is His very word, then we should come to it with humility and awe. This is the only approach that unlocks the treasures of biblical wisdom, and the only one that brings satisfaction and eternal joy.

So, how we approach, read, hear, and consider the Bible has everything to do with our love for God. Because we love Him, we love His every word and look forward to the next one. We cling to, delight in, long for, and treasure up every word, for they are the breath of our Triune God, thundering with the authority of our Father, dripping with the love of our Savior Jesus Christ, and taught to us by the Holy Spirit.

If, as you consider your approach, you feel you are not desirous of bowing to the God of the Bible, I would suggest that you might skip to Chapter Nineteen, "Reading Someone Else's Mail," before you complete the rest of the book. It is my genuine prayer that we will all desire to bow in humility and adoration before the God of the Book.

CHAPTER THREE

THE BOOK IN YOUR HANDS

The impulse to experience the *primitive* New Testament church as closely as possible in their setting necessitated the return of the early Brethren to reliance upon the primitive text, the Bible, as their only rule of faith and practice.[1] For Alexander Mack, this text was Luther's German translation of the Bible, which he obviously considered reliable and precious.[2] At the same time, Mack and other Brethren had expressed interest in the Berleberg Bible, a revised version of the German Bible, printed in 1726.[3]

Here is a practical lesson. Trust the translation, assuming it really is a translation that you have in your hands. Does such trust mean that we will not learn more about the Hebrew, Aramaic, or Greek texts? No, we will, and hope to continue learning more. Does such trust mean that we will not find better ways in the future to express biblical words in contemporary translation? No, we always desire to translate the Bible in accurate and relevant ways. But does our future learning and translation diminish our confidence in the Bible we are reading now? No, not at all.

CHILDLIKE FAITH

I write out of a loving concern for believers who are overwhelmed or confused by the increasing abundance of Bible translations, and they question the validity of their own personal Bible (or maybe any Bible). Be encouraged. There is, in fact, amazing agreement among many translations. We would expect this to be so since the Holy Spirit, who guides history in His sovereign way, also directs the preservation and translation of the biblical text.

Does this imply that there are no bad translations? No, absolutely not. Generally, inaccurate translations tend to be sectarian, cultic, and private.[4] Beware of the group or individual that has to have its own translation.

Does this imply that of the good translations, some may not be better? No, some versions may be considered better, although there can be disagreements among believers concerning which translations are better or best.[5] It is enough for our purposes, among English readers, to mention that Alva J. McClain, first President of Grace Theological Seminary and influencer of the Grace Brethren movement, was partial to the American Standard Version of 1901,[6] the latest version of which is the New American Standard Bible of 1995.

How, then, may we avoid being deceived or confused, and have our confidence affirmed concerning our Bibles? Here are five helps. (1) We may learn some Hebrew, Aramaic, or Greek so that we can check translations of them for ourselves. (2) Whether we learn the biblical languages or not, we should value and consider the input of other genuine believers who have learned them, especially those recognized with the gift of teaching. (3) We may compare various translations rejoicing in agreement, and evaluating points of disagreement. (4) We should be part of the interpretive community—the church—which allows us to read and study the Bible together. This gives us checks and balances, and keeps us from succumbing to private or sectarian interpretations. (5) We may pray for the illumination of the Holy Spirit to guide us.

Likely, the best translation is the one you will actually read and use. So, trust the Bible in your hands.

CHAPTER **FOUR**

THE BOOK AS IT READS

In the first place, what they believe and teach may be comprehended in the statement that they accept the New Testament as their creed and discipline. That is, the New Testament as it is, and not as they would have it, or as they understand it, but as it reads. They believe that the Book is inspired by God, and translated into various languages through His direct instrumentality; that the Book means what it says, and says what it means, nothing more and nothing less, and is not to be added to nor taken from, and will suffer no deviations. That is Tunkerism, briefly but accurately stated. – Henry R. Holsinger[1]

There are many excellent tools for both introductory and more advanced Bible reading and study.[2] It is not the task of this book to join their ranks. Please use them. Standard

CHILDLIKE FAITH

principles of evangelical hermeneutics are agreed upon—literary, grammatical, historical, contextual, purposeful, and more.

One big interpretive principle stood out among the others for the Brethren—observation of the plain sense of Scripture. For many, this one principle was enough. Their desire was to carry out the Bible as it reads. They observed and agreed upon what the Bible says, and then sought to submit to it, obey it, and apply it. They had little interest in complex analysis that clouded the plain sense of a text. They were not given to speculation or formulation that led them into theory, dogma, or creed instead of obedience.[3]

Two of the historic movements of influence come together in this emphasis on the plain sense of the Bible. The first is the Reformation teaching on the clarity, or perspicuity, of Scripture.[4] The Reformed doctrine of the clarity of Scripture means that the message of the Bible itself is self-evident. That does not necessarily mean, however, that all passages are equally clear to the reader or that some passages do not seem more difficult. In other words, if something in the Bible seems unclear, the fault always lies with the reader, not with the Scripture. The second influential movement is the Pietist concept of submissive, heartfelt, immediate, and total obedience.[5] When these two influences combine, the resulting concept is that the Bible is clear in what it says to the believer, and that the believer is accountable to understand what is said and respond in faith and obedience.

It is possible for us to cloak disobedience by claiming ignorance, lack of clarity, confusion, or inexperience, even while the plain sense and expectation of Scripture is staring us in the face. We need to be cautious that we, like the Pharisees and scribes of old, do not "invalidate the Word of God" for the sake of our traditions, backgrounds, preconceptions, theological speculations, cultural accommodations, or political viewpoints (Matthew 15:6). Rather, "the truth will make you free" from such impositions, as you abide in Jesus' Word, follow Him in discipleship, and "know the truth" (John 8:31-32).

May God in His grace free us from our bondage that we may trust and obey the clear, plain sense of the Book as it reads.

SECTION TWO
Childlike Faith

Chapter Five: *Childlike Faith*
Chapter Six: *Understanding with Your Heart*

CHAPTER **FIVE**

CHILDLIKE FAITH

> *Let this be your greatest concern, that all of your sighs and desires be directed toward loving your God (who has created you), and toward loving Jesus Christ (who has redeemed you with His precious blood) with all your heart, all your soul, and all your mind above all things of the world, be it beauty or wealth, yes, whatever may come within your sight or your hearing. Fear God in this love with a <u>childlike heart</u>, contemplate all of His commandments day and night, keep them with a pure heart, let them be your counselors, and pray unceasingly for the Holy Spirit, who will guide you in truth in all of the commandments of God (emphasis added).* – Alexander Mack[1]

The Gospels, positioned at the opening of the New Testament and filled with the words of Jesus, the Head of the church, were influential in defining Brethren discipleship. Luke 14:25-33, which focuses on counting the cost of discipleship, was the passage read at the famous baptism

CHILDLIKE FAITH

in the year 1708 at Schwarzenau, Germany.[2] Matthew 23:8 seems to be the passage from which they derived their preferred name, "Brethren."[3] But page after page in Mack's writing, and in writings over the next century and more after him, make allusions to Matthew chapter 18 as the description of Jesus' teaching concerning living in spiritual community with mutual accountability to one another in church discipline.[4]

Jesus' first words in this important chapter are, "Truly I say to you unless you are converted and become like children, you will not enter the kingdom of heaven. Whoever then humbles himself as this child, he is the greatest in the kingdom of heaven" (Matt. 18:3-4). It is little wonder, then, that childlike faith is a first principle in understanding God's Word.[5]

What is this childlike faith? At least five overlapping characteristics appear as we look at its application. The first characteristic is an *unrestricted trust*. For the Brethren, the question was not so much, "Do you possess faith?" as it was, "Does faith possess you?" Faith drew all of their thoughts, desires, concerns, and conduct into the loving care of Christ. "It was something to be deeply felt."[6] This is the uncompromised, unbetrayed trust of a child.

The second characteristic is the connection of this trust to *love for God*. The Apostle Paul makes this connection often, such as in Galatians 5:6 where he speaks of "faith working through love." Love for God includes a fervent desire to seek His mind, that we may respond to His thoughts and "please Him in all respects" (Colossians 1:10). The evidence of love for God is love for one another (1 John 4:20-21). Alexander Mack, Jr. beautifully reminds us of this connection in Brethren practice:

> Therefore, dear brethren, let us watch, and be careful, and above all *preserve love* for then we will preserve light. For the Spirit of truth testifies in the first epistle of John 2:10, "He that loveth his brother abideth in the light, and there is none occasion of stumbling in him." Then our good God, Who is love purely and impartially, can and will add by degrees, what may be wanting in this or that knowledge (of truth).[7]

So, there is the necessity of childlike faith and love for the understanding of Scripture.

The third characteristic is *immediate obedience*. My wife and I used to teach our children the phrase, "To delay is to disobey." Responding to the words of our Redeemer-Lover-King implies spontaneous, unquestioning, joyful obedience. Jesus said, in John 14:21, "He who has My commandments and keeps them is the one who loves Me."

The fourth characteristic of childlike faith is *adherence to the Bible*. Childlike faith has little interest in speculation, theoretical formulation, or anything which would distract it from obedience to the Bible just as it reads. David's approach in Psalm 131:1-2 is the approach we apply in childlike faith, "O Lord, my heart is not proud, nor my eyes haughty; nor do I involve myself in great matters, or in things too difficult for me. Surely I have composed and quieted my soul; like a weaned child rests against his mother, my soul is like a weaned child within me." As trusting children, we regard God's Word as our safety, security, and sufficiency.

The fifth characteristic is *Christ-centeredness*. In childlike faith, we desire to see Jesus everywhere in

CHILDLIKE FAITH

Scripture, for He is the object of our desire. We read the Bible "with unveiled face, beholding as in a mirror the glory of the Lord" and "are being transformed into the same image," that of Jesus Christ (Romans 8:29), "from glory to glory" (1 Corinthians 3:18).

Childlike faith—characterized by unrestricted trust, love for God, immediate obedience, adherence to the Bible, and Christ-centeredness—this is the key to unlocking the treasure chest of God's Word.

CHAPTER **SIX**

UNDERSTANDING WITH YOUR HEART

My son, if you will receive my sayings and treasure my commandments within you, make your ear attentive to wisdom, incline your heart to understanding; *for if you cry for discernment, lift your voice for understanding; if you seek her as silver and search for her as for hidden treasures; then you will discern the fear of the Lord and discover the knowledge of God. For the Lord gives wisdom; from His mouth come knowledge and understanding. He stores up sound wisdom for the upright; He is a shield to those who walk in integrity, guarding the paths of justice, and He preserves the way of His godly ones. Then you will discern righteousness and justice and equity and every good course. For* wisdom will enter your heart *and knowledge will be pleasant to your soul.*
– Proverbs 2:1-10 (emphasis added)

The methodology of childlike faith is not difficult research or analytical thinking alone. While we need, honor, and appreciate hard-working researchers and excellent thinkers, we heed the warning of the Apostle Paul that "knowledge makes arrogant, but love edifies" (1 Corinthians 8:1). Sometimes the methodology of childlike faith is to look up to the heavens (Genesis 15:5-6), or to the hills (Psalm 121:1-2). Proverbs 2:1-10, quoted above, includes a beautiful listing of methods of childlike faith—receive, treasure, make your ear attentive, cry for, lift your voice for, seek, search. The sum of them all is "incline your heart to understanding."

What does this mean? In Western culture we might have anticipated a statement like "incline your *mind* to understanding," and the Proverbs' statement does not preclude that. Or, we might have expected "incline your heart to *feeling* the impact of this," and the text does not rule that out either. What Proverbs 2:2 does is show us there is no hard distinction in the Bible between mind and heart, or between understanding and feeling. Yes, we *understand* with our *hearts*. That requires us to devote the entire core of our being to understanding biblical truth so that it affects us totally.

It is true that the heart of an unsaved individual is "more deceitful than all else and is desperately sick" so that no one can "understand it" (Jeremiah 17:9). That is why unsaved people do not understand the truths and applications of Scripture. As Paul said, "a natural man does not accept the things of the Spirit of God, for they are foolishness to him and he cannot understand them, because they are spiritually appraised" (1 Corinthians 2:14).

It is equally and powerfully true, however, that when someone trusts in Jesus for salvation and is born-again, God has done a procedure on the heart. Ezekiel 36:26 states it this way, "Moreover, I will give you a new heart and put a new spirit within you; and I will remove the heart of stone from your flesh and give you a heart of flesh." Or, Romans 2:29 refers to this as "circumcision of the heart." Another way for Paul to teach the same truth is that now "we have the mind of Christ" (1 Corinthians 2:16). The Apostle John explains that every born-again believer in Jesus Christ has "an anointing from the Holy One" (1 John 2:20), and that "His anointing teaches you about all things" (1 John 2:27).

Now, look at the promises in Proverbs 2:1-10: you will discern the fear of the Lord; discover the knowledge of God; receive wisdom, knowledge, and understanding; have God as your shield, guard, and preservation; discern every good course. You who feel incapable of high thoughts or rich insights, rejoice! If you incline your heart to understanding you have a promise that you will "discover the knowledge of God." You who have strained your brains on biblical academic research, thinking, and teaching, receive the heartwarming, childlike faith that fills all your valuable and appreciated work with the joy of the love of Jesus. May it be our prayer and experience that "wisdom will enter our hearts and knowledge will be pleasant to our souls."

SECTION THREE

Submissive Obedience

Chapter Seven: *The Obedience of Childlike Faith*

Chapter Eight: *To Change Your Life*

Chapter Nine: *This Book Will Keep You from Sin*

Chapter Ten: *Immediacy*

CHAPTER **SEVEN**

THE OBEDIENCE OF CHILDLIKE FAITH

> *In the subtleties of speculative theology the church takes but little interest. She is chiefly concerned in giving willing and cheerful obedience to the plain, simple commandments of Christ Jesus.* – D. L. Miller[1]
>
> *Mack's basic theme in all his writings is obedience.* – Donald F. Durnbaugh[2]

Growing out of the Proverbs 2:1-10 discussion on understanding with the heart is another observation: God gives His wisdom to the upright, to those who walk in integrity, to His godly ones. That is to say, understanding cannot be separated from obedience. In fact, there is a sense in which obedience, or at least a genuine desire to obey, often precedes understanding. A selection of Bible passages represents this observation.

Second Peter 1:5-8 is an essential description of discipleship qualities or virtues. Eight qualities are listed in ascending order: Faith, moral excellence, knowledge, self-control, perseverance, godliness, brotherly kindness, and love. Notice that moral excellence *precedes* knowledge in this progression. The quality of one's character greatly influences the quality of one's knowledge.

Psalm 25:14 reveals, "The secret of the Lord *is for those who fear Him*, and He will make them know His covenant" (emphasis added). Here, as in Proverbs 1:7, the "fear of the Lord is the *beginning* of knowledge" (emphasis added). While we have noticed that childlike faith produces obedience in love, there may also be the sense in which it produces obedience in fear. A child obeys a parent out of the security of the parent's love, but the same child may obey the same parent even on the same issue out of the realization that the parent is bigger, or stronger, or has authority, so there could be consequences for disobedience. These are not contradictions, they are complementary realities. Every good parent knows this.

Proverbs 3:32 includes, "He is intimate with the upright." Here, moral uprightness in character comes **before** experiencing God's intimacy.

In Ezra 7:10, Ezra *prepared* to know God's truth by *setting his heart* to study the law of the Lord, and to *practice* it, and to *teach* it. Here again, the predisposition to obedience is a prerequisite for understanding.

Finally, our Lord Jesus Himself taught that willingness to obey precedes knowledge. He said, "If anyone is willing to do His will, he will know of the teaching, whether it is of God ..." (John 7:17). Character, obedience, or at least willingness to obey, are all essential to a growing understanding of God's Word.

A beautiful example of this principle is shown in the footwashing event of John 13:1-17. Jesus simply washes His disciples' feet (John 13:3-5). When He comes to Peter, Jesus' intent is questioned (John 13:6). Rather than presenting to Peter a full explanation, Jesus replies, "What I do you do not realize now, but you will understand hereafter" (John 13:7). In this case, participation in obedience clearly precedes understanding. God's truth is comprehended more through obedience than analysis, and more through participation than argumentation.

CHAPTER **EIGHT**

TO CHANGE YOUR LIFE

The purpose of the Bible is not merely to increase your knowledge—it is to change your life. Think of the hundreds of church services, sermons, church and school classes, study groups, etc. which people attend. Maybe some learning takes place—maybe not. But how much real change takes place? I hope in your life discipleship is really happening. Such a life-change approach may be considered *transformational* in contrast to being merely informational.

This is not to be anti-informational. We need good information. Bible reading can be, and should be, informed. Archaeology, history, linguistics, theology, geography, science, and more may all help us read the Bible more intelligently. Guard against the danger of ignorant, uninformed attempts at interpreting Scripture. We need all of the good Bible-content we can get.

However, there is an equal danger to ignorance—pride. Sometimes pride may even be the greater danger. Knowledge can "make arrogant" (1 Corinthians 8:1). One who has "all knowledge" but does not have Christ-like love, is "nothing" (1 Corinthians 13:2). There are far too many examples of those who really know their Bibles but whose lives show little evidence of the fruit of the Holy Spirit (Galatians 5:22-23). There are experts, scholars, teachers, and others who can present massive or unique information without having hearts warmed or lives changed. There are churches, schools, and ministries with reputations and followings, but little interest in pleasing the Lord "in all respects"(Colossians 1:10). There are even those who promote "practical application" of the Bible, but not heart transformation from the Bible. Oh the danger that lurks when intellectual, spiritual, academic, ecclesiastical, or moral pride is present!

So when I open my Bible, I open it with the expectation that it will change me. I open it prayerfully. I pray, not just that I would interpret the Bible, but that the Bible would interpret me. I read it with the anticipation that God has something to say that will transform my life. And I find that He is speaking His sufficient, powerful, life-changing Word.

CHAPTER **NINE**

THIS BOOK WILL KEEP YOU FROM SIN

The life of the believer in Jesus Christ is a life of battle against sin. In an exposition of Romans 8:13, the Puritan pastoral theologian John Owen phrased this, "Be killing sin or it will be killing you."[1] Romans 8:13 is clear that only "by the Spirit" can the believer kill sin. The weapon which the Holy Spirit uses in this battle is "the sword of the Spirit, which is the Word of God" (Ephesians 6:17). Psalm 119:11 puts it, "Your word I have treasured in my heart, *that I might not sin* against You" (emphasis added). Thus, many preachers have turned Owen's phrase into, "The Bible will keep you from sin, or else sin will keep you from the Bible."

Without the Bible, we would not have a clear view of what sin is. Yes, even the Bible acknowledges that all people have an awareness of God and sin through creation (Romans 1:18-32) and conscience (Romans 2:1-16). But the clear and convicting awareness of sin and neediness comes through Scripture. Paul speaks of his own experience with this when he writes, "I would not have come to know sin except through the Law; for I would not have known about coveting if the Law had not said, 'You shall not covet'" (Romans 7:7). It is the proper use of God's Law in the Scriptures to bring us to an awareness of the seriousness of our sin in light of a sensitivity to the holiness of God (1 Timothy 1:8). Jesus Christ, the Living Word (Hebrews 4:13) and the Bible, His written Word, work together as a "living" and "active" sharp "two-edged sword" to "judge the thoughts and intentions of the heart" (Hebrews 4:12). The result is that the believer should cry out with Paul, "Wretched man that I am! Who will set me free from the body of this death?" (Romans 7:24).

From the opposing side, it is the nature of sin to deceive, dull, and deaden. "The flesh sets its desire against the Spirit, and the Spirit against the flesh; for these are in opposition to one another, so that you may not do the things that you please" (Galatians 5:17). Sin will try to keep you unaware of itself. Since the Bible makes us aware of sin so that we can kill it, the continued thriving of sin in the believer depends upon keeping the believer from hearing God in the Bible. Sin will try to make sure that we are too busy, or too tired, or too distracted, or too disinterested to hear God in the Bible. Sin will attempt to make us feel that there are other alternatives than the Bible—lectures, religious services, nature, poetry, music, philosophy, other books, etc. Sin will use anything, even otherwise good things, to keep us from the Bible. Sin will use sports, leisure time, work, entertainment, relationships, or hobbies as easily as it will use lying, adultery, drunkenness, thievery, hatred, or greed.

This does not mean that believers may not enjoy good things in life. God "richly supplies us with all things to enjoy" (1 Timothy 6:17). But it does imply that the enjoyment of all good things comes from surrendering oneself and the use of these things to the Master, Jesus Christ. We must not permit sin to keep us from the Bible, from submitting to the Bible as the lens through which we see and the grid through which we interpret all of life.

It is the Bible that tells the believer that when Jesus died on the cross, the believer died there with Him with reference to sin (Romans 6:1-4, Galatians 2:20). It is the Bible that tells the believer that when Jesus rose from the dead and ascended to heaven, the believer was raised and ascended with Him (Ephesians 1:20-21; 2:4-7). So now the believer has all provision for overcoming sin. It is the Bible that tells the believer that when Jesus returns, the believer will return with Him in glory (Colossians 3:4). And it is the Bible that tells the believer that from eternity past through eternity future, nothing—nothing, nothing, nothing—will ever separate him or her "from the love of God which is in Christ Jesus our Lord" (Romans 8:38-39). Jesus' love for the believer is such that He would not die without you, would not be raised and ascended without you, will not come again without you, and will never be separated from you for a single instant in between and forever.

This message of appropriating the life and provision of Jesus Christ will keep you from sin. It is the Bible that, by the power of the Holy Spirit, is the dynamic that draws the believer to embrace Christ in love and to hate sin. You need no longer yield, or present yourself, to sin. Sin is no

CHILDLIKE FAITH

longer your master—Jesus Christ is! Yield to Him as your sufficiency, joy, treasure, and satisfaction, and you will find the allurements of sin to seem cheap and grow weak (Romans 6:11-14).

All of this provision and more is found in the Bible for the believer. Sin does not want you to see it or feel it. But if you are in Jesus Christ, the provision is yours. So, it is true, "This Book will keep you from sin, or else sin will keep you from this Book."

CHAPTER **TEN**

IMMEDIACY

Quite often the Word of God functions like seed (Matthew 13:19; Mark 4:14). Jesus' parable of the sower instructs us that with reference to the reception of His Word and the growth of His kingdom, there are various soils and seasons. Sometimes response to truth comes slowly.

But this parable should not discourage us from believing that there does come a moment when fruit breaks out. To change the metaphor, the Lord declares, "Is not My Word like fire, and like a hammer which shatters a rock?" (Jeremiah 23:29). Obviously there are times when God speaks His Word with immediacy. It spreads and burns like a wildfire or brings a smashing blow like a hammer. The Word of God, like a sword razor-sharp on both sides, radically and rapidly "pierces as far as the division of soul and spirit" (Hebrews 4:12).

This concept of immediacy does not bypass the need for prayer, patience, diligence, study, or research. Nor does it negate valid principles of hermeneutics, use of biblical languages, or insights from culture, archaeology, or travel to biblical lands. All are necessary, helpful, and valid. But God is not limited by our methods and efforts.

CHILDLIKE FAITH

Furthermore, not everyone has access to all of these tools, training, or travel.

God can illuminate His Word to the scholar and the uneducated alike. Sometimes the needed insight comes after long periods of meditating on God's Word, while other times it comes as a flash just at the right moment. God can break through in the midst of rigorous academic discipline, or in prayerful Bible reading.

Some of God's people are held in bondage by thoughts or their own limitations. Here are some examples:

- "I'll never have the time, money, or ability to go to college or seminary."
- "I don't have the ability to learn Greek or Hebrew."
- "I am not that intellectually inclined."
- "I don't have the money or time to take a trip to biblical lands."
- "I can't afford a bunch of commentaries and books."
- "I'm not sure that God has anything to say to me."

These kinds of limitations tend to reinforce notions that the Bible is not accessible, clear, understandable, or practical. But the Bible is, in reality, all of these and more. Remember the statement of Acts 4:13, "Now as they observed the *confidence* of Peter and John and understood that they were uneducated and untrained men, they were amazed, and began to recognize them as having been with Jesus" (emphasis added).

As you read your Bible, the Holy Spirit can quicken His Word to you. The Holy Spirit can take you, through the pages of God's Word by faith, into biblical lands, language, and culture. We should not allow limitations, real or perceived, to prevent us from experiencing all that God desires for us to experience in our knowledge of Him on each page of His Book.

I have personally been blessed with opportunities for education and travel, some beyond what I would ever have anticipated. I am grateful for them all. But it is evident to me, increasingly evident, that the value of each opportunity is only in proportion to what God shows me from His Word.

This notion of immediacy is not intended for us to use the Holy Spirit as an excuse not to read, study, prepare, or work hard. It is intended, however, to say to us, *Expect God to break through to you in His Word, and bring to you at the right time and in the right way what you need.* After all, it is Jesus Himself who said, "The words that I have spoken to you are spirit and are life" (John 6:63).

SECTION FOUR

Communal Interpretation

Chapter Eleven: *The Church—Understanding in Community*

Chapter Twelve: *Hearing—Word, Spirit, and Community*

Chapter Thirteen: *No Other Creed*

CHAPTER **ELEVEN**

THE CHURCH—UNDERSTANDING IN COMMUNITY

The interpreting community for the Anabaptists was the congregation of believers meeting together around Scripture to learn how to live as disciples. – Stuart Wood Murray[1]

The biblical teaching of the priesthood of every believer (1 Peter 2:1-10; Revelation 1:6) is essential to a proper understanding of the church. Jesus Christ builds His church (Matthew 16:18) "as a spiritual house for a holy priesthood" (1 Peter 2:5). When Jesus brought His church into existence as the unique expression of the people of God for this age at Pentecost, He did it through the pouring out of His Spirit (Acts 2:1-13) and the proclamation of His Word (Acts 2:14-36; Joel 2:28-32; Psalm 16:8-11; Psalm 132:11; Psalm 110:1).

The Holy Spirit and the Word create the church. This is an important, and for some, a radical understanding. Both unbelieving critics and institutional religious authorities assert that the church created the Bible, not that the Bible created the church. After all, was it not Christians who wrote the New Testament? And were there not "church councils," culminating in The Council of Carthage (397 AD), which determined the twenty-seven canonical New Testament books?

Yes, but the critics and hierarchicalists have forgotten a highly significant point—the statement of Psalm 119:89, "Forever, O Lord, Your Word is settled in heaven." Jesus Christ is the One who canonized the Old Testament (Matthew 5:17-18; 21:42; Luke 24:25-27) and the New Testament (John 14:26; 16:12-15; Matthew 10:14, 40). Church councils, to the extent that they had any validity at all, could have at best agreed with, or ratified, what Jesus had already created and determined. Jesus is Lord, not any ecclesiastical hierarchy. It is not, as such, that the Bible is the Book of the church, but rather that the church—the assembly of genuine believers—is the church of the Book.

In stark contrast to the biblical teaching of the priesthood of the believer, look at this section from the Roman Catholic "Dogmatic Constitution on Divine Revelation" promulgated at Vatican II:

> *It is not from sacred Scripture alone that the Church draws her certainty about everything which has been revealed. There both sacred tradition and sacred Scripture are to be accepted and venerated with the same sense of devotion and reverence. Sacred tradition and sacred Scripture form one sacred deposit of the word of God, which is committed to the Church... The task of authentically interpreting the Word of God, whether written or handed*

> *on, has been entrusted exclusively to the living teaching office of the Church, whose authority is exercised in the name of Jesus Christ... It is clear, therefore, that sacred tradition, sacred Scripture, and the teaching authority of the Church, in accord with God's most wise design, are so linked and joined together that one cannot stand without the others, and that all together each in its own way under the action of the Holy Spirit contributes effectively to the salvation of the souls.*[2]

It is clear in this constitution that Roman Catholicism does not agree that the Bible alone is the Word of God. The document indicates that for Vatican II, the Word of God equals the Bible plus Catholic tradition. It is also clear in this constitution that interpretation of either the Bible or tradition is "exclusively" the privilege of those in the Office of the Magisterium, the "teaching office of the Church." Thus, Catholicism would take your Bible from you.

But Catholicism is not alone in stealing the Bible from believer–priests. What is happening when someone says, "My church believes this," instead of saying, "Let's look together at what the Bible says"? Is this not giving a church or denomination some magisterial authority? Or when traditions, styles, or preferences become emotionally as or more important than the Bible, what has become of the Bible and the believer? Or when interpretations based on cultural assumptions or traditions override the plain sense of the text, has not the Bible been lost?

Just as human reason is not to be over the Bible or equal to the Bible, but submitted under the Bible, so the church is not over the Bible or equal to the Bible, but submitted to the Bible. The Bible creates, forms, guides, and preserves the church—we must never reverse this.

This discussion has massive implications for our understanding of Paul's words in 1 Timothy 3:15, "...the household of God, which is the church of the living God, the pillar and support of the truth." In what sense is the church "the pillar and support of the truth"?

The Vatican II "Constitution on Divine Revelation" would imply that 1 Timothy 3:15 means that the truth cannot function apart from the authority, traditions, and offices of the church. Rejecting such a view on grounds already discussed, may we simply ignore Paul's statement? No, the reality remains that the church is "the pillar and support of the truth."

Homer A. Kent, Jr. interprets Paul's statement as meaning that the church "upholds in the world the truth which God has revealed to men."[3] If we take the word *church* (*ekklesia*) as it is rather than attaching organizational or hierarchical baggage to it, the idea is that the assembly of God's people upholds the truth of Scripture. God's believer-priests assembled in community are together to understand, defend, communicate, and spread His Word.

In reacting against hierarchical authoritarianism, we must not collapse into a privatized individualism. While we profit from our personal reading of the Scriptures, we need the entire believing community to contribute to accurate interpretation. Hermeneutics, the science and art of interpretation should be done together. In that sense, we never really read the Bible alone. We are part of a believing community—formed by the Word.

The Church—Understanding in Community

It is the continual task of the church to understand, systematize, and clarify the teaching of Scripture for its own time.[4] As the Holy Spirit continues His teaching ministry in the community of believers (notice that the word "you" throughout 1 John 2:27 is plural, not singular), more and more insights from more and more believers bring more and more clarity of understanding. On this point, Anabaptists, Pietists, and Puritans were all in agreement.[5] There is powerful and beautiful protection from error in this. Since the Holy Spirit is "clear, undivided, and without contradiction,"[6] if believers are mutually submitted to the same Spirit and to one another, then they will be likewise.

In a church in which I fellowshipped, worshipped, and served some years ago, someone came to our Bible class one day with great enthusiasm over a recent insight into Scripture. This dear friend in Christ exclaimed, "The Lord has shown me the meaning of the 'abomination of desolation' in Daniel 9:27. During the tribulation period there will be one bomb to destroy each nation. Get it?—a 'a-bomb-a-nation.'" Now in spite of the fact that there are several errors in this statement and the result is a fanciful and preposterous notion, no damage was done. Why? Because this individual was part of a believing community that immediately brought correction and guidance in love and balance. Plus, we all had a good laugh. There is safety, protection, and spiritual profit in community.

This identifies the church, then, as a hermeneutical community. Reading and studying the Bible in the context of a fellowship of believers requires a core desire to live a life of discipleship. Experiencing the church as a hermeneutical community will impact the way classes, small groups, sermons, seminars, and other ministries are done. "Designating the local congregation as the 'locus of interpretation' was arguably the most important and distinctive Anabaptist contribution to sixteenth-century hermeneutics or biblical interpretation."[7]

CHAPTER **TWELVE**

HEARING—
WORD, SPIRIT,
AND COMMUNITY

How do we hear God in the Bible? There are three vital means of help for us as we hear, read, and study the Word of God.

The first means of help is through the text of the Word itself. The nature of the Bible is that it is the Word from God to struggling, persecuted, suffering people. Whether throughout the history of Israel or the history of the church age, struggle, persecution, and suffering make up the experience of God's people. That is why a section like Romans 8:18-39 is precious to so many of us, or why Psalms is favorite personal reading.

There is no rich understanding of the Bible without discipleship, and there is no discipleship without the struggle of self-denial, cross bearing, and cost-counting (Luke 9:23-26; 14:26-35). Therefore, as the believer experiences the struggle of discipleship, the Bible is designed in such a way that we may personally insert ourselves into the text. The Word of God is unchanging and eternal, so we enter it with our changing and temporal situations and always find grace to sustain us. What is eternal is always relevant. We have the text living in us through continued meditation upon it (Joshua 1:7-9, Psalm 1:2), and we live in the text by faith. The Word of God does not help some people because it is not "united by faith" in them (Hebrews 4:2). As the believer and the text are "united by faith," the believer hears God. What a joy to situate ourselves, to locate ourselves, to *indwell* in a sense,[1] the narratives, the epistles, the poetry, the metaphors, and other figures of speech. In this way, we hear God interpreting us in the text!

The second means of help is the work of the Holy Spirit. Romans 8:5 informs us, "For those who are according to the flesh set their minds on the things of the flesh, but those who are according to the Spirit, the things of the Spirit." What are "the things of the Spirit" in Romans 8:5? The only other text where we find this phrase is in 1 Corinthians 2:14, "But a natural man does not accept *the things of the Spirit* of God" (emphasis added).

We ask again what the phrase means. In the context of 1 Corinthians 2, we find immediately in verse 13 that these "things of the Spirit" are *words*. They are not "words taught by human wisdom" but rather "taught by the Spirit." Examination of the fuller context confirms that these words are the words of Scripture (verse 16). In other words, the Bible records the very "thoughts of God." Now, the only way we can know these "thoughts of God" is by "the Spirit of God" (verse 11). The work of the Holy Spirit, in this regard, is to cause us to understand Scripture. He gives us understanding of the very "thoughts of God" that "we may know the things freely given to us by God" (verse 12). Therefore, we can say, "We have the mind of Christ" (verse 16).

The joy of hearing by the Spirit is an issue in Galatians 3:1-5 as well. In this passage, Paul equates receiving the Spirit and His work with "hearing with faith" (Galatians 3:2, 5). He amplifies that the believer did not receive the Spirit, and does not continue to receive the Spirit's work, "by the works of the Law" (Galatians 3:2, 5). We do not enjoy the Spirit's work in us by our own attempts, strivings, thoughts, and self-efforts. Rather, we continue to receive all that He desires to open up to us from His Word by *trusting Him*, by "hearing with faith."

As we put these passages together, then, we observe that...
- believers set their minds on the things of the Spirit
- the things of the Spirit are the Words of Scripture
- the words of Scripture are the very thoughts of God
- the thoughts of God are freely given to us by the Spirit
- believers hear these thoughts by receiving them in faith.

What thrilling grace it is to hear and know the very thoughts of God!

The third means of help for us in hearing God in His Word is the community of believers. We began to think about this in chapter eleven. I want to expand our thoughts by suggesting seven ways through which the believing community might help us hear God in His Word.

The first way the community of believers can help us is by *connecting us to the primitive, apostolic church and to church history*. How does the community connect us to the primitive, apostolic church? Carl F. Bowman expresses this thought beautifully:

> *Equally important, the Spirit was eternal and unchanging. If truth had been revealed to the earliest apostles, that truth would not have changed one iota in the generations and centuries since. Christian unity thus required believers to be of* one mind, one faith, and one practice, *even on matters that would seem petty or trifling to outsiders. And the Christian community of the present age, as nearly as possible, was expected to mirror the apostolic community depicted in Scripture. Simply stated, unity had two faces, one contemporary and one transgenerational; it linked brother with brother* and *brother with the ancient Brethren. Its timeless sweep embraced every generation of "saints" right back to the apostolic era. The Brethren even came to refer to themselves as "ancient brethren," a clear expression of this sense of timeless Christianity."*[2]

Once we have settled our desire for genuine discipleship and embraced the believing community, it is only normal and proper to feel the eternal connection to the apostolic community and desire to mirror it in our cultural setting as closely as possible. This happens through communal reading of the New Testament.

How does the community connect us to church history? On the day of Pentecost (Acts 2:1-47), Jesus' prayer in John

17:20-21 was answered, expressly, that all believers of the entire church age were made one in Him. So Paul could say in 1 Corinthians 12:13, "For by one Spirit we were *all* baptized into one body..." Because we are one in Christ, we can fellowship with people we have never met and perhaps who lived centuries before us. How? Not through some kind of transcendent metaphysics—of course not (such would be demonic). But, through reading their books, commentaries, articles, and biographies, or hearing of their stories and reputations, we can empathize with them and feel like we know them. In this way, we learn from them and profit by sharing their experiences and insights, which help us hear God as well.[3]

The second way the community of believers can help us is by *including excellent scholars and teachers* in the community.[4] That is significant to mention because in chapter eleven we attempted to establish that the locus for biblical interpretation is the local church, not in the academy. This is not to suggest, however, that there is no role for the academy in the process of biblical interpretation. In fact, to the extent that churches have failed to be interpretive communities as they ought, they owe colleges, seminaries, and research ministries an overwhelming debt of gratitude for carrying out their responsibilities. But the true value of the academy should be in its functioning as part of the church, in its servant-role to believing communities. In this way, we all may profit from the excellent contributions and insights of these skilled researchers and teachers.

The community of believers can help us in a third way by *including mission agencies/missionaries* in the community. As will be made clearer in chapter sixteen, we desperately need those with a Great Commission perspective to remind us constantly that the Bible is a missional Book. To miss the missional emphasis on most pages of the Bible would be to miss the heartbeat of God. Missionaries and agency leaders can be greatly used of God to help churches keep pace with their Great Commission calling.

A fourth way the community of believers can help is closely related to the third, and this is by *including global dimensions* in the interpretive process. Believers from diverse social, racial, economic, political, and cultural backgrounds[5] are all invited to the hermeneutical table of the community. In our communal Bible interpretation, we do not need or desire merely to reaffirm our own conventional ideas. We also need and desire to have our presuppositions challenged or expanded by different perspectives. This is not to suggest that we become open to error or compromise, but it does remind us that we each can be limiting the Bible from within a mono-cultural trap if we are not careful. Missionaries can also help us with this. Every nation on earth needs to be contributing to, as well as receiving from, the interpretive process.

The fifth way the community can help is by *including diversity* within its own setting. Beyond the global dimensions, there is also diversity of age, gender, employment, marital status, parental status, and more within each local assembly. Old and young, female and male, single and married, without children and with children, blue collar and white collar—all are needed to contribute in our understanding of Scripture. We need to realize and utilize more the transgenerational nature of a church family. Childlike faith teaches us that the Lord will use a child to cause us to hear His voice (Matthew 18:1-2; Isaiah 11:6).

The sixth way the community of believers can help is to *maintain a commitment to expository Bible teaching and preaching*. In our promotion of reading and studying the Word, we cannot afford to lose the blessing of *hearing* the Word (Romans 10:17; Revelation 1:3). Believers need to hear—we must hear—the Bible exposed and explained on a regular frequency in the context of a believing, worshipping community. This is what forms the church, so that without it there is no church.

And the seventh way in which the believing community can help us hear God is by maintaining biblically-sanctioned *physical-instructive experiences*. One example of a physical-instructive experience in Scripture is walking. Deuteronomy 6:4 prescribes walking (as well as sitting, reclining, or standing) as an excellent venue for teaching children the Word of God. In Luke 24:13-35, Jesus walked alongside two disciples from Emmaus and used this as a teaching opportunity. "Then beginning with Moses and with all the prophets, He explained to them the things concerning Himself in all the Scriptures" (Luke 24:27). Later these disciples said to one another, "Were not our hearts burning within us while He was speaking to us on the road, while He was explaining the Scriptures to us?" (Luke 24:32). These men had a heartwarming "hermeneutical moment" in the midst of a physical-instructive experience.

When Jesus arrived at Emmaus with these disciples, He engaged in another physical-instructive experience—eating. It was when Jesus took bread, blessed it, broke it, and gave these disciples some that "their eyes were opened and they recognized Him" (Luke 24:31). The Lord's Supper, or Love Feast (1 Corinthians 11:17-22; Jude 12), is an eating physical-instructive experience commanded for the church

CHILDLIKE FAITH

to perpetuate. In the Love Feast, Jesus Himself offers to come alongside and dine with us, and for us to dine with Him (Revelation 3:20).

The Bread and Cup is also a physical-instructive experience in which the Lord's death is proclaimed until He comes (1 Corinthians 11:23-26). In John 13:7, 17 Jesus indicates to Peter that Footwashing is a physical-instructive experience from which learning takes place and blessing is received. This is why Jesus called it a sign, or representation ("example"), and instructed it to be perpetuated among His disciples (John 13:14-17). The church should not overlook the opportunities to use these physical activities as biblical teaching events in which we hear God.

CHAPTER **THIRTEEN**

NO OTHER CREED

Because of their aversion to formal creeds and confessions, it is often said that the early Brethren were noncreedal, with the assumption being drawn that they were tolerant of individual differences and "ever open" to new light from the Holy Spirit. Such an assumption could not depart more dramatically from their original uncompromising biblicism. Rather than calling the Brethren noncreedal, it is much more historically accurate to say that they adopted the entire New Testament as their creed. They were literalists in the sense that clear scriptural authority for a particular ordinance or practice caused them to adhere to it rigidly, demanding that all true Christians do likewise. On the other hand, if the New Testament was silent on something, they were skeptical and hesitant to adopt it. Thus, far from being uncritically open to new illumination, they believed that all new light had to be measured against old

CHILDLIKE FAITH

light (Scripture) to test its worth. – Carl F. Bowman[1]

Through careful study of both the Scriptures and early church history, the original "Tunkers" sought to form a body of believers founded on the principle that the Bible alone is sufficient, not only in matters of doctrine, but also in determining the structure and practices of the church. – Tom Julien[2]

We rejoice in the truth of the sufficiency of Scripture. The Bible includes and speaks to every family, language-group, and nation (Revelation 5:9, 7:9). It covers all time, from eternity to eternity, from creation to consummation (Psalm 90:1-2; Genesis 1:2; Revelation 22:12-13). The Bible has a message and plan for every place (Isaiah 34:1; Acts 17:26), and for every creature and thing (Colossians 1:20; Revelation 5:13). In the sense of the Bible's own purposes for itself, you cannot think of anything for which it is not sufficient. Through the "precious and magnificent promises" of Scripture and the "divine power" of the grace of Christ and the moving of His Spirit, we affirm that the Lord "has granted to us *everything* pertaining to life and godliness" (2 Peter 1:2-4, emphasis added). And so we gladly sing with the hymn writer:

> *My faith has found a resting place,*
> *not in device nor creed.*
> *I trust the Everliving One,*
> *His wounds for me shall plead.*

> *I need no other argument,*
> *I need no other plea.*
> *It is enough that Jesus died,*
> *and that He died for me.*[3]

But we need to acknowledge that the truth of the sufficiency of Scripture can be misunderstood and misapplied. In the interest of bolstering our confidence in the sufficiency of Scripture, here are four things that the sufficiency of Scripture does *not* mean.

First, the sufficiency of Scripture does not mean that every individual, private interpretation of Scripture is right. While we reject creedalism, we do understand that sometimes creeds have been formed for essentially good reasons. The fear of fanciful interpretations, heresies, and dangerous trends or movements can tempt us to feel that Scripture is not able to take care of itself and requires our help to defend it against error. Creeds, then, have often been formulated as corrections or protections affirming biblical truth. This is valid so far. Creedalism becomes a problem, however, when over time the creed becomes "the reference point for belief as well as for further research and reflection," which means "in *practice* creeds become the spectacles through which the Word is read and interpreted."[4]

Thus, creedalism is a lack of confidence in the sufficiency of Scripture. We *are* concerned about confronting heresy and error, but we trust the Bible to be enough to deal with this as the Spirit of God uses the Word in the context of the believing community. In this sense, we also identify creedalism as possible laziness because it can shallowly rely upon the creed instead of doing the ongoing, hard work of

CHILDLIKE FAITH

the community in thinking and applying Scripture in new circumstances.

Second, the sufficiency of Scripture does not mean that the Bible is designed to work in an individualized, privatized manner apart from the believing community (although it is so powerful that it can). We affirm again the necessity of obedience and discipleship in community. Both the Bible and the church have been designed by God to interact with one another under the authority of the Holy Spirit. We need to be participating in a truthful community in order to read the Bible well. We value spiritual mothers and fathers who serve as our guides, and we delight in the prospect of being a mother or father for others (1 Thessalonians 2:5-12).

Third, the sufficiency of Scripture does not mean that the Bible is designed to have information concerning every matter about which anyone is ever interested. For example, if you want to build a motorcycle, you will not find a schematic diagram in the Bible showing you how to build it. That is not the purpose of the Bible; however, this does not render the Bible insufficient. The Bible does have something to say about your motives, attitudes, and actions as you build or ride your motorcycle (or do anything else). All of life is to be lived under the Lordship of Jesus Christ for the glory of the Father (1 Corinthians 10:31).

Fourth, the sufficiency of Scripture does not mean that the Bible will solve all your problems without your believing and obeying it. Remember, for the Word to be profitable it must be "united by faith" in the hearer (Hebrews 4:2).

And so, we worship the Lord in the sufficiency of His Word, along with David.

*The law of the Lord is perfect, restoring the
    soul;*
*The testimony of the Lord is sure, making
    wise the simple.*
*The precepts of the Lord are right, rejoicing
    the heart;*
*The commandment of the Lord is pure,
    enlightening the eyes.*
*The fear of the Lord is clean, enduring
    forever;*
*The judgments of the Lord are true; they are
    righteous altogether.*
*They are more desirable than gold, yes, than
    much fine gold;*
*Sweeter also than honey and the drippings of
    the honeycomb.*
Moreover, by them your servant is warned;
In keeping them there is great reward (Psalm 19:7-11).

SECTION FIVE

Tranformational Separation

Chapter Fourteen: *Not Conformed to this World*
Chapter Fifteen: *Separation Without Isolation*

CHAPTER **FOURTEEN**

NOT CONFORMED TO THIS WORLD

> *"Love not the world, neither the things that are in the world, If any man love the world, the love of the father is not in him" (I John 2:15). Nonconformity was grounded in the conviction that true faith had transforming power; it changed the believer, shifting his or her point of orientation to new and higher ground. This was the positive side of nonconformity. It was understood that a byproduct of this positive renewal would be a negative tension with the surrounding temporal order. Becoming "alive to Christ" implies experiencing a "death to the world." In Mack's words, the true church "is dead to sin" and "raised again to newness of life in Christ Jesus" Yet it is still "walking outwardly in this evil world, in a state of humiliation." – Bowman*[1]

The first four principles for approaching the Bible (Biblical Authority, Childlike Faith, Submissive Obedience,

CHILDLIKE FAITH

and Communal Interpretation) all serve together to demonstrate that the Bible is only rightly understood through the working of God the Holy Spirit. But, there is another spirit—a differing spirit, an enemy spirit—at work in the world. The principle of Transformational Separation highlights the reality that the believing community, in essence opposed to the enemy spirit in every surrounding culture, cannot hear God in Scripture when it has an ear tuned to the frequency of the wrong spirit.

Jesus describes the reality of two opposing ways. One way is popular and accommodating; "For the gate is wide and the way is broad that leads to destruction, and many are those who enter through it" (Matthew 7:13). The other way is not so popular and is less accommodating; "For the gate is small and the way is narrow that leads to life, and there are few who find it" (Matthew 7:14). Jesus says, "Enter through the narrow gate" (Matthew 7:13). These contrasts appear throughout the New Testament; destruction or life, darkness or light, lawlessness or righteousness, Satan or Christ, unbeliever or believer, idolatry or church, unclean or clean (2 Corinthians 6:14-18).

The church, by definition (*ekklesia*), is an assembly of "called-out ones." The principle of non-conformity to the temporal spirit of the age is, then, a consistent plea for the church to live like what it is. "Therefore, 'come out from their midst and be separate,' says the Lord, and 'do not touch what is unclean,' and I will welcome you" (2 Corinthians 6:17).

In Romans 12:2, the contrast appears again. One may be "conformed to this world" or "transformed by the renewing of your mind," but not either, nor both. There is no neutral, spiritual demilitarized zone. Nor will spiritual fence-straddling be possible without moving to one side or the other. One may operate in the wisdom of "the rulers of this age," or "God's wisdom" (1 Corinthians 2:6-8). The side you have a taste for reveals your identity. One may function according to conformity to the world spirit—its thoughts, definitions, values, perspectives, goals, and desires (1 John 2:16). Or, one may enjoy the beauty of a transformed life by a mind renewed through the thoughts, values, perspectives, goals, and desires of the Bible. Which do you desire— worldliness or renewal?

Moses made the choice "to endure ill-treatment with the people of God" rather than "to enjoy the passing pleasures of sin" (Hebrews 11:25). Have we embraced the value that there is eternal satisfaction and joy in identification with the community of believers that will never be experienced in the world's participation in its temporal pleasures? Moses also chose to consider "the reproach of Christ greater than the treasurers of Egypt, for he was looking to the reward" (Hebrews 11:26). Have we come to feel that there is such future, ever-increasing reward in Jesus Christ that even to be reproached for Him is a greater treasure and prize than all the riches of the world?

If we *desire* the value of identification with God's people and the worth of the treasure which is in Christ, we will gladly "present our bodies" to Him as a "living and holy sacrifice" (Romans 12:1). We will be like a man who finds a treasure in a field, and in order to obtain the treasure "from *joy* over it he goes and sells all that he has and buys that field" (Matthew 13:44). Or, we will be like a merchant who finds one extraordinary "pearl of great value" and "went and sold all that he had and bought it" (Matthew 13:45).

What is the value of one eternal insight from the Bible? It is worth more than all the words on all the pages of all the

CHILDLIKE FAITH

other books ever written. A persecuted believer may give up everything else, just to clutch a torn page from the Bible. But when on that page the believer sees the beauty of Jesus Christ and believes the grace of His promises, it is worth everything.

We who have all the pages of the Bible have the ovewhelming privilege of hearing God in every line. Surely this is worth separating from all that would cloud our vision, dull our senses, or stop our ears. Surely no price could be too high to pay for this breathtaking pearl.

CHAPTER **FIFTEEN**

SEPARATION WITHOUT ISOLATION

The positive side of non-conformity and separation is transformational. Transformational Separation prevents the church from becoming "of the world" (John 17:16), thus preserving its primitive identity. In the words of Alva J. McClain, "[When] the Church loses its 'pilgrim' character [then] the sharp edge of its divinely commissioned 'witness' is blunted. It becomes an *ekklesia* which is not only in the world, but also *of* the world."[1] So separation should keep the church healthy and effective.

But, unfortunately, there has been a negative side to separation that has not been transformational (at least not in a healthy way). From the late 1700s through the mid 1800s, legalism crept into the Brethren movement in a sad fashion. Strangely, in the interest of non-conformity, the church "developed a conformity that was to distinguish it in days to come."[2] Plain dress, avoidance of home decorations, abstaining from voting or holding public office, distrust of education, criticism of musical instruments or singing in parts instead of unison—these and other matters demonstrate "the narrow and restricted viewpoint of the Brethren of this time."[3] The famous German printer, Christopher Sauer, remarked as early as 1725 that the Brethren had "erected a fence around themselves."[4] This self-protective, ingrown isolationism clouded vision and dulled the cutting edge of Great Commission witness.

It is in one context, one prayer, that Jesus prays *both* that His disciples are "not *of* the world" *and* that He has "sent them *into* the world" (John 17:14-18, emphasis added). While Jesus clarifies the necessity of separation from worldliness, He expects the purpose of separation to maximize penetration into the world, not isolation from it. The Great Commission includes going into the world (Mark 16:15; John 20:21).

At least four contrasts may be observed between transformational separation and isolational separation. First, isolation tends to reveal *pride*, while transformation tends to reveal *humility*. A group in isolation can develop a "fortress mentality" and may begin to feel that it is the only group that is right or true. Out of pride, then, such a group becomes rigid, fixed, unforgiving, and less than gracious. A transformational community maintains humility (James 4:6) in order to reach, include, and forgive people.

Second, isolation tends to advance *fear*, while transformation tends to advance *love*. In isolation, concerns over the behavior of others in the group, or the loss of young people, or compromise of any kind, can easily slip into legalistic control. As the controllers become more controlling, others become more silent, fearful, and ingrown. All kinds of sins, problems, perversions, or inadequacies become hidden or covered-up in such an environment. This is a serious problem, for, as Proverbs 28:13 instructs us, "He who conceals his transgressions will not prosper, but he who confesses and forsakes them will find compassion." Also, fear places constraints upon legitimate joys. What do you do, or where do you go, if you enjoy singing a part while only unison singing is permitted?

Transformation, in contrast, addresses the concerns in love. Consider 1 John 4:18 in this light, "There is no fear in love; but perfect loves casts out fear, because fear involves punishment, and the one who fears is not perfected in love." Transformation encourages the participants in the believing community to sing their parts. Transformation encourages joy, grace, help, acceptance, and forgiveness in love.

A third contrast is that groups in isolation tend to become *static*, while groups in transformation are *dynamic*. To state the principle that believers should dress in a way that is not worldly and reflects biblical values is excellent. But to cause this principle to mean that believers must dress in the same way believers dressed in the 1600s, 1700s, 1800s, 1950s, or you name when or how, is to turn an excellent principle into unthinking, static legalism. The same thought applies to numerous issues—building plans, musical styles, orders of worship, outreach methods, and so forth.

The dynamics of transformation imply, rather, that we must continually do the hard work of thinking about how we apply unchanging biblical truth in changing cultural situations. Primitive church believers living out Christlike holiness in one era or culture do not look identical to primitive church believers in other eras or cultures. Yet we are all believing and applying the same commands and precepts. The static approach seems to remain stuck in continuing to fight yesterday's battles, and winning them in a self-protective, fixed, codified manner. The dynamic approach understands that there is always a fresh battle to fight and win with the "sword of the Spirit, which is the Word of God" (Ephesians 6:17).

Fourth, while a community in isolation is likely to *avoid biblical responsibility*, a community in transformation tends to *embrace biblical responsibility*. A community in isolation may ignore the questions and challenges of its youth. It tends not to evangelize and grow. It may be likely to avoid being the "salt of the earth" or the "light of the world" or the "city set on a hill" (Matthew 5:13:15). It often fails in its responsibility to "shine before men in such a way that they may see [their] good works" (Matthew 5:16). Transformational communities embrace these responsibilities.

It is fair to say that after decades of severe persecution, the Pietist-Anabaptist communities retreated into enclaves of self-protective isolation that "had a progressively diminishing impact on culture at large."[5] Yet, it also seems fair to say that earlier their vision was for a mission intended to transform culture.[6] "They were concerned ... to follow Jesus in all of life, in the social and political as well as the religious spheres. Out of this concern they insisted on religious freedom, developed a new economics, refused to take the oath, and did not participate in warfare. In [their] context, these beliefs, protests, and alternative practices in effect made [them] 'socially revolutionary' in some sense."[7] A shining example is that in an era when many other American Christians and Christian leaders owned slaves, the Brethren from the start consistently condemned the practice.[8]

The Pietist movement in general interpreted eschatological Scripture passages from a futuristic, pre-millennial approach.[9] Philip Jacob Spener held to such an interpretation, positing, according to David Larsen, "a two-fold parousia or double coming of Christ" (i.e. a pre-tribulational rapture and pre-millennial second coming of Jesus).[10] Spener was mentor to August Hermann Francke who founded the University of Halle and so, influenced Nicholas Ludwig Von Zinzendorf, Jonathan Edwards, John Wesley,[11] as well as Gottfried Arnold and Ernst Christoph Hochmann Von Hochenau. The latter influenced Alexander Mack[12] who at least taught the imminent return of Jesus Christ.[13] Sometimes it has appeared that those who are future-oriented tend to ignore their personal and social responsibilities in the present, and even tend to be isolationist. But the impetus of prophetic Scripture is always to obedience and involvement (Titus 2:11-15; 1 John 3:3; 2 Peter 3:10-14). A future-focus on Christ in faith will always lead to transformational activity if rightly understood. Such faith is not escapist.

Alva J. McClain has said this instructively and beautifully:

> ...We know that *some* physical diseases have been conquered, *some* wars have been prevented, *some* hazards to life and safety have been eliminated, *some* years have been added to the brief span of human life, *some* social and political evils have been corrected. If this be so, why then should there not be an age when *all* wars will be stopped, *all* diseases cured, *all* the injustices of government, rooted out, and a *full* measure of years added to human life? Why should there not be an age in which all such unrealized and worth-while dreams of humanity will at last come true on earth? If

there be a God in heaven, if the life which He created on the earth is worth-while, and not something evil *per se*, then there ought to be in history some worthy consummation of its long and arduous course.[14]

The premillennial philosophy of history makes sense. It lays a Biblical and rational basis for a truly optimistic view of human history. Furthermore, rightly apprehended, it has practical effects. It says that life here and now, in spite of the tragedy of sin, is nevertheless something worth-while; and therefore all efforts to make it better are also worth-while. All the true values of human life will be preserved and carried over into the coming kingdom, nothing worth-while will be lost. Furthermore we are encouraged in the midst of opposition and reverses by the assurance that help is on the way, help from above, supernatural help—"Give the king thy judgments, O God … In his days shall the righteous flourish … all nations shall call him blessed" (Ps. 72:1, 7, 17).[15]

With the Bible as our "Sword of the Spirit," the believing community functions as the conscience of society, speaking God's Word to our culture. We must bring God's Word to bear on issues of sanctity of life, sexual purity, sanctity of marriage, economic or political oppression, racial injustice, or whatever the issues of the day may be. God's people are to be the "city set on a hill." So we also read our Bibles well when we read with a transformational understanding of both the church and society.

SECTION SIX

Missionary Dynamic

Chapter Sixteen: *Reading Like a Missionary*

CHAPTER **SIXTEEN**

READING LIKE A MISSIONARY

The Progressive movement, developing from about 1851-1882 and culminating in the identification of the Brethren Church in 1883, pulled the Brethren movement out of isolationism and legalism.[1] Vision was again being restored.

By the time of the annual conference of 1900, the Lord raised up a number of people ready to join Jacob C. Cassel in the establishment of a missionary society.

Here are some of his words from that conference:

> The missionary outlook for the twentieth century, whether hopeful or hopeless, altogether depends upon the standpoint of one's vision.
>
> We have reached a period in the world's history in which God's dear children believe the prophecies, feel the force of the commission, with the world open, the means of com-

munication and transportation developed, with money and men in abundance, and back of all this the promise of the presence of Jesus to whom all power is committed in heaven and in earth. Surely the outlook is altogether hopeful.

If the evangelization of the world is to you what the north star is to the sailor, if you will always take your bearings from that God-focalized center, your responsibility will be met.[2]

What Cassel says about fulfilling our Great Commission responsibility is also true about our approach to the Bible—it "altogether depends upon the standpoint of one's vision." When believers with a missional mindset "are infused with vision, they see things that others do not see."[3] They see people, opportunities, needs, ways, and means, and they also see insights in Scripture. Keeping the evangelization of the world as a "north star" will also help us to hear God in the Bible. There are at least seven ways that reading the Bible with a missional vision can help us.

First, a missional vision reminds us to read the whole Bible as *a record of missionary activity*. God the Father is a missionary God, Israel is a missionary nation, Christ is a missionary Savior, the Holy Spirit is a missionary Spirit, and the church is a missionary church.[4] As such, everything we see in Scripture has some relationship to God's coming, going, or sending on His redemptive mission—the culmination of His Kingdom for His glory.

Second, reading the Bible like a missionary reminds us to see the whole Bible as *a message to be proclaimed*, not just studied and understood. We feel the value and urgency of the biblical message for all nations. Throughout Scripture Christ is revealed and His Gospel confirmed, and we know that people desperately need this message. When we read to proclaim and study to teach (Ezra 7:10), we experience the blessing that the teacher usually learns more than the student.

Third, a missional vision causes us to see the *New Testament as a missionary document.* The New Testament is a missionary document in the sense that it was written by apostles for evangelistic (John 20:31) and discipling (2 Timothy 3:16-17) purposes. But, it is also a missionary document in that much of it may be seen as a manual for missionary activity. For example, the instruction by Jesus to the apostles in the Gospels should be viewed as missionary leadership training.[5] We see missionary recruitment (Matthew 4:18-22), recruitment methodology (Matthew 9:37-38), and missionary sending (Matthew 10:1). We see evangelistic principles modeled (John 4:3-42). We see discipling enacted (John 13:1-17), explained (John 13-16), and prayed for (John 17). The Book of Acts is a descriptive, historical manual for missionaries, and the Epistles of Paul show the development of missionary processes and maturity in the formation of churches, especially when they are read in the order in which Paul wrote them.[6]

Fourth, missional Bible reading reminds us that our biblical *interpretations must be practical.* How can I explain the message to others if I do not know what to do with it in my own experience? If I cannot explain it, do I really understand it? The vision of a missionary includes the vision for others being able to apply the Scripture and do what it says. This takes Bible reading out of the theoretical realm and places it in the arena of practice.

Fifth, a missional vision necessitates a heart for accurate *Bible translation*. We desire every person to have access to the Bible in her or his own language. This can improve our own Bible reading so when we attempt to explain or translate a word into another culture or language, we sometimes discover that the word has more or different significance than we had realized. Thus, we can all continue to learn from one another through linguistic and cultural diversity in the community of believers and grow in our understanding.

Sixth, missional Bible reading causes us to see biblical *details as significant*. It is missionaries who most often remind us, for example, that God's stated purpose in setting up and taking down geo-political boundaries is so that people from every people-group "would seek God" (Acts 17:26-27). It is missionaries who remind us that these geo-political entities are *countries*, but that *nations* are the people groups. So when missionaries see the detail of every "nation" represented before the heavenly throne in Revelation 5:9 and 7:9, they see a detail that makes the heart pound with excitement, even while others miss it.

Who and where are the people-groups today who began in the table of nations in Genesis 10? How does this relate to the people-group I am trying to reach? Does this relate to Bible prophecy? Missionaries find such details interesting and helpful, even when they are not always certain of the answers.[7] Do genealogies really matter? Even though it can be overwhelming at times, ultimately we will see that every detail has significance.

And seventh, missional vision can remind us that we grasp the significance of the prophetic word best *in terms of evangelism*. We understand what it means to "hasten" the coming day of God (2 Peter 3:12) only from a missional perspective in view of the purpose of God's patience (2 Peter 3:8-9). When we read Paul's massive view of God's sovereignty in Romans 9-11, we weep with him over the lostness of his kinsmen and ours (Romans 9:1-3) and pray with him for their salvation (Romans 10:1). We hear the details and the urgency of tone in Jesus' words, "This gospel of the kingdom shall be preached in the whole world for a witness to all the nations, and *then* the end will come" (Matthew 24:14, emphasis added).

If God is a missionary God and a mission of redemption is on His heart, then we must read the Bible with a missional vision if we are to hear God's heart in His Word.

SECTION SEVEN
Sufficient Grace

Chapter Seventeen: *The Promise of the Future*
Chapter Eighteen: *Every Promise in the Book Is Mine*
Chapter Nineteen: *Reading Someone Else's Mail*

CHAPTER **SEVENTEEN**

THE PROMISE OF THE FUTURE

Having emerged from the deadness of isolationism into the vibrancy of freshly infused missionary vision, the Brethren had a new set of battles to fight. By the early 1900s, there were teachers in their midst who were endorsing liberal theology, causing the Brethren to find themselves in "a Brethren version of the Modernist-Fundamentalist controversy."[1] Though the main body of believers was orthodox in belief, because there was little expository Bible preaching with depth and breadth, there also developed "an absence of emphasis on the doctrine of the pure grace of God with all its implications."[2]

Some, divorcing Pietism from its Reformed background, felt that Pietism had to be Arminian in theology.[3] The liberal, or modernist, side had some adherents who would not affirm the full inspiration, inerrancy, and infallibility of Scripture,[4] others who embraced theistic evolution,[5] and even more who felt that their Pietist heritage meant that Bible doctrine must be downplayed in favor of personal experience.[6] These were just a few of the issues.

CHILDLIKE FAITH

On the fundamentalist side, "there was a growing movement, particularly under the teaching of Dr. McClain, that wanted to identify Brethrenism with a more Calvinistic, premillennial, fundamentalism."[7] This became known as the "Grace Group" and led to the forming of Grace Theological Seminary and the Fellowship of Grace Brethren Churches. Without belaboring the history any further, we now turn to some of the influences of the Spirit of God in the Grace Movement, particularly in the teaching of Alva J. McClain.

The "Message of the Brethren Ministry," which McClain had a major role in formulating along with twenty-four others, begins by stating a Grace Brethren motto, "The Bible, the whole Bible and nothing but the Bible."[8] Thus, a solid belief in the sufficiency of Scripture was reaffirmed. Under the heading, "The authority and integrity of the Holy Scriptures," the "Message" continues:

> The ministry of the Brethren Church desires to bear testimony to the belief that God's supreme revelation has been made through Jesus Christ, a complete and authentic record of which revelation is the New Testament; and, to the belief that the Holy Scriptures of the Old and New Testaments, as originally given, are the infallible record of the perfect, final and authoritative revelation of God's will, altogether sufficient in themselves as a rule of faith and practice."[9]

We continue to approach the Bible with humble and full confidence in it as the inerrant, authoritative Word of God. From this we must never veer.

The Promise of the Future

McClain stressed the magnitude of God's grace in his commentary, *Romans: The Gospel of God's Grace*. Consider his comments on Romans 3:24.

> How much does it cost to be justified? Not a thing! "Being justified without a cause; being justified for nothing." You did not pay a cent for it. But that doesn't mean that it was cheap. Now the next phrase. How was it done? "By His grace!" He first of all says that we had nothing to do with it, then he turns around and shows God did it. It was the unmerited, undeserved favor of God![10]

Or, in Romans 5:2:

> But "being justified by faith, we have" a standing. *We stand*, and our standing is in Christ Jesus. In Christ Jesus is the only place any man will ever be able to stand. How is that standing maintained? *By grace*. Any man who tries to stand in his own works, his own character, his own righteousness, will fall. Grace is the only thing that can maintain his standing. I praise God for His grace this day, and you ought to, too."[11]

This emphasis on grace caused McClain to hold to the doctrine of the security of the believer. In his book on Romans, in chapter sixteen entitled "Preservation: Kept Securely in Christ Jesus", McClain puts it this way:

> There remains just one more question that can arise: will this divine method of

> justification and sanctification last? The eighth chapter of Romans was written to answer that question, and the whole burden of the chapter is this: *if you are in Christ Jesus, you are safe!* Justification and sanctification in Christ will endure. So then, we might say that the theme of Romans 8 is *security*, or to put it broadly, *preservation*."[12]

The believer, hearing of the promises of God for the eternal future, can appropriate by faith the secure power of those promises for living today in spiritual confidence.

Out of his concern to interpret the Bible as it reads, McClain also taught that there are literal promises to literal Israel, as well as literal promises to the literal church age. He says concerning Romans 11:1-10,

> There is a school of thought in Christendom which says that in the church God has fulfilled everything in the Old Testament and there is no future for the Jew as a nation.[13] But the opposing view is that God has set Israel aside for an age, and at some future time (in the next age) God will fulfill to the latter every promise He has made to Israel as a nation. That second view is the right one.[14]

From this vantage point of literal promises for Israel's future, McClain sees prophetic significance in the return of Jews to the land of Israel. Comparing Romans 11:15 with Ezekiel 37, McClain writes:

There is a stirring in the "bones" in this twentieth century. Many of Israel have gone back, but "there is not breath in them," that is, spiritual life. They are going back to their land unconverted. But even though that is the picture, the word comes to the prophet, "Son of man, these bones are the whole house of Israel." That is the divine interpretation. "What shall the receiving of them be but life from the dead?"[15]

The powerful thrust of McClain's classic *The Greatness of The Kingdom* is its demonstration that there are hundreds of biblical promises to Israel which have not yet been fulfilled, but must be and will be fulfilled in the future. Such promises include the abolition of all military warfare, complete social justice, proper valuation of every legitimate interest of human life, Jerusalem as the capital of the world, language barriers removed, beneficial climatic changes, changes in the animal world, the disappearance of physical disease and deformity, the Jewish Temple rebuilt on the Temple Mount in Jerusalem as the world center for worship, and so forth.[16] The believer may accept these promises regarding God's future for Israel with confidence.

If God has a future plan to be fulfilled for Israel, part of the encouragement is that just as He will fulfill His plan for Israel, He has a plan for the church which He is fulfilling and will fulfill in this age. "For I am confident of this very thing," says Paul, "that He who began a good work in you will perfect it until the day of Christ Jesus" (Philippians 1:6). In this regard, McClain sees eternal security as protecting the believer from all "wrath to come" (1 Thessalonians 1:10 and

CHILDLIKE **FAITH**

5:9), including the wrath of God (Revelation 6:16-17) to be poured out in the future tribulation period.[17] McClain is so careful to preserve this security of grace that he delineates ten full pages of arguments for the pre-tribulational removal of the church from earth to heaven, each argument with supporting subpoints.[18] The design of his view is not escapist, but grace-oriented.

All of this really matters in our Bible reading because so much of the Bible is in the future tense. The power for our present is located significantly in the security of our future. Just read a passage like Romans 8:11-39 and observe how much is personally prophetic about our future, and extend your observation to much of the New Testament. The doctrine of sufficient grace helps us hear the promises of God for our present and our future, and to rejoice that the fulfillment of these promises is and will be sure.

CHAPTER **EIGHTEEN**

EVERY PROMISE IN THE BOOK IS MINE

By God's all-sufficient grace, every statement of the Bible has something in it that applies to the believer. The full scope and breadth of Scripture guarantees that it is sufficient to provide wisdom for every life situation.

Having previously stressed that numerous promises are specifically directed to Israel, it may seem strange to state now that the promises are for church-age believers as well. Yes, many promises are directly and literally for Israel, and the church has not replaced Israel, so the promises must be read with that distinction in mind. While there are ample passages written directly to the church, even the promises to Israel can be applied *indirectly* to church-age believers once they have been correctly understood for Israel. There are at least four ways these promises can be understood as relating to the church.

First, we see Jesus the Jewish Messiah everywhere in Scripture. Jesus Himself said concerning the Jewish Scriptures "You search the Scriptures because you think that

CHILDLIKE FAITH

in them you have eternal life; *it is these that bear witness of Me* (John 5:39, emphasis added). So we are blessed in seeing Jesus in the entire Bible.

Second, we learn spiritual lessons from God's direct blessings to Israel. We see Jesus Christ in Moses' faithful leadership (Hebrews 3:5-6). The Sabbath is for all believers a rest of faith in Jesus Christ (Hebrews 3:7-4:16). The Levitical priesthood actually speaks of Jesus (Hebrews 7:11-28) as well as the priesthood of all believers in this age (Hebrews 13:15; 1 Peter 2:5). The Tabernacle was a "copy and shadow of the heavenly things" (Hebrews 8:1-5) which are now ours in Christ (Ephesians 1:3). The Law itself is fulfilled for us and in us in the perfect life and sacrificial death of Jesus (Hebrews 10:1-18) and the continual working of the Holy Spirit (Romans 8:3-4). The Temple is instructive for the church (1 Corinthians 3:16-17). Jerusalem has spiritual value for believers in this age (Hebrews 12:18-24). The Jewish Feasts all find their fulfillment in Jesus Christ and have heartwarming application for believers (1 Corinthians 5:7-8; Acts 2:1; 1 Corinthians 15:52; Hebrews 10:19-22; etc.).

Third, we see spiritual examples in many Israelite and Jewish events. Concerning the Exodus and the wilderness wanderings, Paul writes in First Corinthians 10:6, "Now these things happened as examples for us ..." The great "hall of faith" in Hebrews 11 is filled with Old Testament and Jewish examples for us.

Fourth, in Christ, Gentile believers are "grafted in" to Israel's blessings and promises (Romans 11:17, 19). "Therefore, be sure that it is those who are of faith who are sons of Abraham" (Galatians 3:7). Church-age believers have received the "circumcision which is of the heart by the Spirit" (Romans 2:29). In this way, the promises, the covenants, the land, and the Kingdom become ours indirectly through Israel's future. We bless Abraham and his seed, knowing that we in turn will be blessed (Genesis 12:3). We rejoice in the good of Israel and "pray for the peace of Jerusalem," knowing that those who love her will "prosper" (Psalm 122:6-7).

Alva J. McClain's counsel is edifying when processing this:

> In this connection I would like to encourage Christians who delight in finding the Lord Jesus Christ upon every page of Scripture. Do not permit yourselves to be frightened by those overcautious souls who cry against what they call "too much typology." Doubtless there are some things which may properly be catalogued as "types" and others not. But whatever you may call it, it is the privilege and highest duty of the Christian to discover and behold the face of the Lord Jesus in Scripture—everywhere! Far better to break a few rules of classical hermeneutics than to miss the vision of His blessed face.
>
> We need only one caution—let us be sure that what we find is always true to the historic revelation of the Son as recorded in the New Testament. With this safeguard, there is no end to what we may find in the inspired record of the infinite and incarnate Son of God. And by finding Him throughout Scripture, we shall be finding the perfect will of God in the wonderful context of His grace. For grace reigns "through righteousness

unto eternal life by Jesus Christ our Lord" (Romans 5:21).[1]

We can add our "Amen" to the little Sunday School chorus:
> Every promise in the Book is mine,
> > every chapter, every verse, every line.
> I am living in His grace divine –
> > every promise in the Book is mine.[2]

We approach the whole Bible, then, with the confidence of 2 Corinthians 1:20, "For as many as are the promises of God, in Him they are yes; therefore also through Him is our Amen to the glory of God through us."

CHAPTER **NINETEEN**

READING SOMEONE ELSE'S MAIL

I sincerely hope and pray that this book helps and encourages you in your understanding of the Bible.

It is possible, however, that you still find yourself uninterested in understanding the Scriptures. Or perhaps you have tried reading the Bible, but you just don't seem to "get it." Maybe what you do understand from the Bible you do not like. Possibly you just do not desire God or a Book that claims to be from Him. You could even be a technical biblical scholar, but not have an interest in God Himself or the life-giving power of His words.

You need to know that the Bible is primarily the message from God to those who have trusted exclusively in His Son Jesus Christ. Such people treasure Jesus and prize the Bible as His Word. The Bible calls people who have not entered into such a relationship with Jesus "natural." That may not sound bad, but it is serious because the Bible says that "a natural man does not accept the things of the Spirit of God, for they are foolishness to him; and he cannot understand them, because they are spiritually appraised" (1 Corinthians 2:14).

Because the words of the Bible can only be "spiritually appraised," the hearer or reader must be tuned in to God's spiritual frequency in order to understand them. Otherwise, the experience can be a little like reading someone else's mail. You know what the words mean, but at the same time you don't know what they mean. It becomes confusing because it was not written to you.

So the big question is, "How do I get tuned in to the right spiritual frequency?" Or, to put it in the other image, "How can I know that the Bible is for me, so that I am reading mail written to me?"

First, if you do not have the interest or desire, I can only recommend that you call out to God to give it to you. Keep asking God until you have the desire. The Bible says that "he who comes to God must believe that He is, and that He is a rewarder of those who seek Him" (Hebrews 11:6). So, seek Him.

Second, once you have the desire, you need to realize it is what the Bible calls "sin" that keeps you tuned to the wrong spiritual frequency. Sin is the violation of God's perfect character as reflected in His Law. The Ten Commandments are part of God's Law. They can be found in the Bible in Exodus 20:1-17. Have you ever failed to keep any of these commands? That is evidence of sin. For example, have you ever considered anything in your life, even yourself, to be more important than God? Have you ever spoken God's name cheaply or profanely? Have you ever dishonored your parents? Have you ever hated or murdered anyone? Have you ever participated in sexual activity of any kind outside of the context of your own marriage (defined as one man and one woman married for life)? Have you ever stolen anything? Have you ever told a lie? Have you ever coveted anything that belonged to someone else?

Violation of any of these, or hundreds of other commands of God, indicates that you are in the condition called "sin." The Bible says that "all have sinned and fall short of the glory of God" (Romans 3:23). Sin is a condition that you cannot escape. You cannot free yourself from it—you are not able to do so. The Bible says that sin is a master that owns you (Romans 6:16) and that "the wages of sin is death" (Romans 6:23). Sin keeps you from being tuned in to God's spiritual frequency. It keeps you separated from God. Ultimately its outcome is death (see Romans 6:21) and eternal punishment (see Matthew 25:46) in eternal fire (see Matthew 25:41), in total darkness (see Matthew 25:30) separated from God, all people, all joy, all goodness, all love, all relationships, and all light forever and forever and forever.

Is there any remedy for this desperate condition? By now you should want the remedy as much as you want your next breath. If you do not, you need to keep asking God to give you the desire.

Third, because you cannot free yourself from your sin-condition, the Bible says that the remedy must be a free gift. "The free gift of God is eternal life in Christ Jesus our Lord" (Romans 6:23). Because the gift is free, it cannot be earned, deserved, or even cooperated with. It can only be received. It comes, not as a result of our works or efforts, but through receiving alone (see Romans 4:5). To be freed from the sin-condition requires a release from the condition. This is what the Bible calls "forgiveness of sins" (see Luke 24:47). Forgiveness can only be granted to you as a gift (see Acts 5:31). Only God can forgive sin (Mark 2:7).

Fourth, how is the gift of forgiveness effective? How does it work? The Bible says that God "the Father has sent the Son to be the Savior of the world" (1 John 4:14). The Son is Jesus, the Messiah of Israel and Redeemer for the world. Jesus has always, eternally, been God (see John 1:1-3). When He was born in Bethlehem, Israel (probably about 4 B.C.), He "became flesh" (see John 1:14). This means He is the God-Man, fully God and fully human. This is absolutely unique. There are no other God-Men; there never have been and never will be. "There is one God and one mediator also between God and men" (1 Timothy 2:5).

Jesus performed miracles—He healed the sick, restored the sight to the blind, and raised the dead, to name a few (see Matthew 11:5). His miracles demonstrated Who He is, God the Messiah. He is a unique combination of power and compassion, sorrow and joy, grace and truth (see John 1:17-18). Though Jesus was tempted in every conceivable way humans can be tempted, He never sinned (see Hebrews 4:15). He was rejected by men, being put to death by hanging on a cross (see Acts 5:30).

The Bible makes the death of Jesus the center of the discussion concerning the forgiveness of sin. His death was a substitution for you in complete satisfactory payment for your sin. "Christ ... died for sins once for all, the just for the unjust, so that He might bring us to God" (1 Peter 3:18). God "demonstrates His own love toward us, in that while we were yet sinners, Christ died for us" (Romans 5:8). He had no sin of His own, so His death was for our sin.

You should be marveling in humble appreciation over the beauty of the life and gracious provision of the death of Jesus for you. If you are not, call out to God to give it to you.

Jesus is "declared the Son of God with power by the resurrection from the dead" (Romans 1:4). The core of what the Bible calls "gospel," or "good news," is "that Christ… died for our sins according to the Scriptures, and that He was buried, and that He was raised on the third day according to the Scriptures" (1 Corinthians 15:3-4). That Jesus was raised and is alive is verifiable (see 1 John 1:1-3). Jesus was "delivered over because of our transgressions, and raised because of our justification" (Romans 4:25). Because He is alive now, He can forgive sin and save you from your sin condition. Consider the power, love, and wonder of Jesus Christ.

Fifth, how do we personally receive the provision for forgiveness that Jesus accomplished? The answer is the title of this book—*Childlike Faith*. Jesus said, "Unless you are converted and become like children, you will not enter the kingdom of heaven" (Matthew 18:3). Childlike faith is believing one whom you trust. The Bible says, "But as many as received Him, to them He gave the right to become children of God, even to those who believe in His name" (John 1:12). "Believe in the Lord Jesus, and you will be saved" (Acts 16:31). That is, you will be freed from your sin-condition.

In the very instant that you place your trust in Jesus Christ as your Savior, He makes you alive with Him, forgives you from all sin (past, present, and future), cancels out all condemnation against you, taking it "out of the way, having nailed it to the cross" (see Colossians 2:13-14). He gives you the free gift of eternal life (Romans 6:23).

Why not quietly trust Jesus now? If this is your desire and you are trusting Him, you may wish to express your trust in prayer. If you are not sure of what to say in your prayer, maybe something like this will help:

> *Lord Jesus, you are perfect and sinless, but I have been sinful. Thank You for dying in my place, for suffering and bleeding for my sins. Thank you for rising from the dead and being here right now to save me. I trust You, Jesus. I trust in You alone, not in myself or my works but in You and You alone. You are my Savior. I love You.*

Once you have trusted in the Lord Jesus Christ, there are some things you will begin to *know*. This is good news, and it is the point of this chapter. You will be able to "*know* that you have eternal life" (1 John 5:13). You will *know* that the Holy Spirit is in you and that you are a child of God (Galatians 4:6). Quite spectacularly, and here is the whole point, because you now have the Holy Spirit as your Instructor, you will *know* the truth of the Bible (1 John 2:20, 27). The Bible is now *your* mail. You are tuned in to God's frequency. You love God and His Word. You long for and delight in His insights for you in the Bible, and you will gain much help and joy from the truthful community of believers in Jesus Christ to which you now belong. Our transformation into the image of Christ is a maturing process, revealing that childlike faith is not immature childishness (Ephesians 4:14).

Such are the benefits, now and forever, of childlike faith.

ENDNOTES

Chapter 1: *Coming to the Book*
1. Carl F. Bowman, *Brethren Society: The Cultural Transformation of a "Peculiar People"* (Baltimore: The John Hopkins University Press, 1995), p. 27.
2. Alva J. McClain, *Romans: The Gospel of God's Grace* (Chicago: Moody Press, 1973), p. 194.
3. Bowman, p. 26.
4. *The Complete Writings of Alexander Mack*, William R. Eberly, ed. (Winona Lake: BMH Books, 1991), p. 39.
5. Bowman, p. 26.
6. Bowman. p. 27.
7. Bowman, pp. 46-47.
8. Bowman, p. 5.
9. See Mark A. Noll, *The Rise of Evangelicalism: The Age of Edwards, Whitefield, and the Wesleys* (Downers Grove: InterVarsity Press, 2003), pp. 60-75. See also Stanley J. Grenz, "Nurturing the Soul, Informing the Mind" in *Evangelicals and Scripture* (Downers Grove: InterVarsity Press, 2004), p. 27. Also note, since the end of the Thirty Years' War in 1648, each German principality was to choose either Catholicism, Lutheranism, or the Reformed church as its legal state church. See David R. Plaster, *Finding Our Focus: A History of the Grace Brethren Church* (Winona Lake: BMH Books, 2003), pp. 2-4.
10. The word "stepchildren" reflects the wording in the helpful title by Leonard Verduin, *The Reformers and their Stepchildren* (Grand Rapids: Eerdmans, 1964).
11. Bowman, p. 27.
12. Eberly, p. 11.
13. Eberly, p. 27.
14. Eberly, p. 83.
15. Quoted by Bowman, p. 36.
16. Eberly, p. 113.

CHILDLIKE FAITH

17. Norman B. Rohrer, *A Saint in Glory Stands: The Story of Alva J. McClain* (Winona Lake: BMH Books, 1986), pp. 117-118.
18. Plaster, p. 8.
19. Plaster, pp. 55-56.
20. Plaster, pp. 55-69.
21. Plaster, p. 124.
22. Rohrer, pp. 117-118.
23. I realize I have deliberately been sketchy, hitting some points to show trends, so historians may be wondering "what history?"

Chapter 3: *The Book in Your Hands*

1. Bowman, p. 26.
2. Eberly, p. 7.
3. Plaster, p. 26.
4. An example would be the *New World Translation* of the Jehovah's Witnesses.
5. If you want help in evaluating English translations, you may want to consult Robert L. Thomas, *How To Choose a Bible Version* (Glasgow, Scotland: Christian Focus Publications, 2004).
6. Rohrer, p. 125.

Chapter Four: *The Book as It Reads*

1. H. R. Holsinger, *History of the Tunkers and The Brethren Church* (Lathrop, California: privately printed, 1901), p. 232.
2. Introductory: Richard Mayhue, *How to Interpret the Bible For Yourself* (Winona Lake: BMH Books, 1986); R. C. Sproul, *Knowing Scripture* (Downers Grove, Illinois: InterVarsity Press, 1977); Tremper Longman III, *Reading the Bible With Heart and Mind* (Colorado Springs: NavPress, 1997); Gordon D. Fee and Douglas Stuart, *How to Read the Bible for All Its Worth* (Grand Rapids: Zondervan, 2003); Rick Warren, *Personal Bible Study Methods* (Foothill Ranch, CA: privately published—contact Pastors.com., 1981). More advanced: Grant R. Osborne, *The Hermeneutical Spiral* (Downers Grove, Illinois: InterVarsity Press, 1991); Milton S. Terry, *Biblical Hermeneutics* (Eugene, Oregon: Wipf and Stock Publishers, 1999); previously published by Hunt and Eason, 1890); Henry A. Virkler, *Hermeneutics: Principles and Processes of Biblical Interpretation* (Grand Rapids: Baker Book House, 1981); David S. Dockery, Kenneth A.

Matthew, and Robert B. Sloan, eds., *Foundations For Biblical Interpretation* (Nashville: Broadman and Holman, 1994).
3. Bowman, p. 28. See also James H. Lehman, *The Old Brethren* (Elgin, Illinois: Brethren Press, 1976), p. 47.
4. R. C. Sproul, pp. 15-17. An excellent discussion.
5. Bowman, p. 27.

Chapter Five: *Childlike Faith*
1. Eberly, p. 100.
2. Plaster, p. 7.
3. Plaster, p. 9.
4. Eberly, pp. 33, 34, 66, 70, 79, 92.
5. See also Eberly, p. 53.
6. Bowman, p. 27.
7. Alexander Mack, Jr., *Rites and Ordinances* (Ashland, Ohio: Century Printing, 1939), p. 98. Also, Bowman, p. 28.

Chapter Seven: *The Obedience of Childlike Faith*
1. D. L. Miller, "Brethren or Dunkards" in *The Brethren's Tracts and Pamphlets, Setting Forth the Claims of Primitive Christianity*, Vol. I. (Mt. Morris, Illinois: Brethren's Publishing Co., 1892), p. 3.
2. Donald F. Durnbaugh, "The Genius of the Early Brethren," *Brethren Life and Thought* 4 (Spring 1959), p. 6.

Chapter Nine: *This Book Will Keep You from Sin*
1. John Owen, "Mortification of Sin in Believers" in *The Works of John Owen*, Vol. VI (Edinburgh: The Banner of Truth Trust, 1967), p. 9.

Chapter Eleven: *The Church—Understanding in Community*
1. Stuart Wood Murray, *Spirit, Discipleship, Community: The Contemporary Significance of Anabaptist Hermeneutics* (Ph.D. thesis, Oxford: The Whitefield Institute, 1992), pp. 420-422.
2. "Dogmatic Constitution on Divine Revelation" in *Documents of Vatican II* (New York: Guild Press, 1966), pp. 117-118.

CHILDLIKE FAITH

3. Homer A. Kent, Jr., *The Pastoral Epistles* (Chicago: Moody Press, 1958), p. 145 (Revised edition also available. Winona Lake, IN: BMH Books, 1995).
4. M. Eugene Osterhaven, *The Faith of the Church* (Grand Rapids: Eerdmans, 1982), p. 1. See also Peter Toon, *The Development of Doctrine in the Church*: (Grand Rapids: Eerdmans, 1979), p. 105.
5. See Stanley J. Grenz, "Nurturing the Soul, Informing the Mind" in *Evangelicals and Scripture* (Downers Grove: Inter Varsity Press, 2004), pp 25-27.
6. Bowman, p. 30.
7. Sara Wenger Shenk, *Anabaptist Ways of Knowing* (Telford, Pa.: Cascadia Publishing House, 2003), p. 48.

Chapter Twelve: *Hearing—Word, Spirit, and Community*

1. For a similar approach from an Anabaptist perspective see Shenk, pp. 53-54.
2. Bowman, p. 30.
3. Shenk, p. 52.
4. Shenk, p. 52.
5. Shenk, p. 52.

Chapter Thirteen: *No Other Creed*

1. Bowman, p. 29.
2. Thomas Julien, "Brethrenism and Creeds" in *Grace Theological Journal* (Winona Lake, IN: Grace Theological Seminary; Volume 6, No. 2, Fall 1985), p. 379.
3. Lidie H. Edmunds, 19th Century, "No Other Plea."
4. Julien, p. 375.

Chapter Fourteen: *Not Conformed to this World*

1. Bowman, p. 42.

Chapter Fifteen: *Separation Without Isolation*

1. Alva J. McClain, *The Greatness of the Kingdom* (Winona Lake, Indiana: BMH Books, 1959), p. 439.
2. Plaster, p. 38.
3. Plaster, p. 39.

Endnotes

4. Quoted in Bowman, p. 43.
5. Shenk, p. 54.
6. Shenk, p. 54.
7. Marlin Miller, *Anabaptism: Neither Catholic Nor Protestant* (Waterloo, Ontario: Conrad Press, 1973), p. 78.
8. Bowman, p. 81.
9. David L. Larsen, *The Company of Hope* (Bloomington, Indiana: Author House, 2004), pp. 146-161.
10. Larsen, p. 155.
11. Noll, pp. 61-64.
12. Bowman, p. 4. See also Plaster, p.5.
13. Eberly, p. 73, 97.
14. McClain, p. 530.
15. McClain, p. 531.

Chapter Sixteen: *Reading Like a Missionary*

1. See Plaster, chapter four.
2. In Tom Julien, *Seize the Moment* (Winona Lake, Indiana: Grace Brethren International Missions, 2000), p. 9.
3. Julien, p. 17.
4. One can hardly rehearse this without acknowledging the seminal messages by John R. W. Stott, "The Biblical Basis of Declaring God's Glory" in David M. Howard, ed. *Declare His Glory* (Downers Grove: Inter Varsity Press, 1977), pp. 31-91.
5. This is the beauty of the classic by A. B. Bruce, *The Training of the Twelve* (Grand Rapids: Kregel Publications, 1971).
6. See Robert L. Reymond, *Paul: Missionary Theologian* (Fearn, Ross-shire, Scotland: Christian Focus Publications, 2000). For a monumental analysis of Old Testament background to New Testament mission and a commentary on the development of mission in the New Testament, see Eckhard J. Schnable, *Early Christian Mission*, two volumes (Downers Grove: Inter Varsity Press, 2004).
7. For excellent and helpful work on the who and where of some of the nations, see Edwin M. Yamauchi, *Foes from the Northern Frontier* (Eugene, Oregon: Wipf and Stock Publishers, 2003), and *Africa and the Bible* (Grand Rapids: Baker, 2004). See also *The Timechart of Biblical History* (Edison, NJ: Chartwell Books, 2005).

CHILDLIKE FAITH

Chapter Seventeen: *The Promise of the Future*
1. Plaster, p. 90.
2. Plaster, p. 90.
3. Plaster, p. 98.
4. Plaster, p. 90
5. Plaster, p. 92.
6. Plaster, p. 98. For a fuller account of this era, see Plaster, pp. 89-146. If you are unfamiliar with some of these terms, Plaster is helpful in defining them.
7. Plaster, p. 97.
8. Plaster, p. 92.
9. "The Message of the Brethren Ministry" (adopted at conference in 1921 and endorsed in 1938), article 2.
10. McClain, *Romans*, p. 107-108.
11. McClain, *Romans*, p. 125-126.
12. McClain, *Romans*, p. 159.
13. Such a view has more recently come to be called "replacement theology," in which Israel is replaced by the church.
14. McClain, *Romans*, p. 196.
15. McClain, *Romans*, p. 200.
16. McClain, *The Kingdom*, pp. 224-254.
17. McClain, *The Kingdom*, p. 465.
18. See McClain, *The Kingdom*, pp. 463-475. Interaction with these arguments is outside the scope of this project. The point here is that McClain saw the pre-tribulational rapture as necessary both to his literal hermeneutic *and* his view of grace and eternal security.

Chapter Eighteen: *Every Promise in the Book Is Mine*
1. Alva J. McClain, *Law and Grace* (Winona Lake, Indiana: BMH Books, 1954), pp. 67-68.
2. Source unknown.

Also Available from BMH Books

www.bmhbooks.com
or call (toll-free) 1-800-348-2756

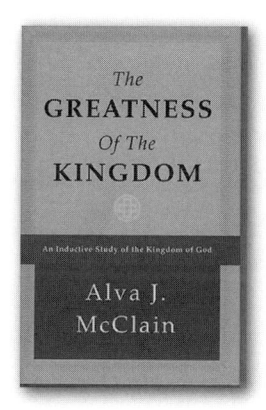

The Greatness of the Kingdom
By Dr. Alva J. McClain

This classic penetrating analysis of the Kingdom of God as taught in both the Old and New Testaments, has just been republished in a handsome hardback, dust jacket edition by BMH Books of Winona Lake, IN. The 556-page masterwork, which retails for $24.99, is available online or by calling 1-800-348-2756. Dr. McClain, who was the founding president of Grace Theological Seminary, was a member of the Scofield Reference Bible Revision Committee and a charter member of the Evangelical Theological Society.

556 pages, hardback, dust jacket
ISBN #0884690113
$24.99 retail

Finding Our Focus
By Dr. David Plaster

The late Dr. Homer A. Kent, Sr. documented the history of the Grace Brethren Fellowship from 1708 to 1958 and then, in a revision, up to 1972. The succeeding years witnessed significant changes in the Fellowship, and Dr. David R. Plaster has carried the history up to 1992 and mentions events and personalities up to 2003 that reflect the re-discovered vision and mission of the FGBC. Dr. David R. Plaster served for twelve years in pastoral ministry in Pennsylvania and Indiana before joining the faculty of Grace Theological Seminary in 1984. He is currently the Vice President for Academic Affairs and Professor of Theology at Grace College and Seminary.

189 pages, trade paperback
ISBN #0884692442
$12.95 retail

Heroes Who Live On, Volume 2

These short vignettes on 13 "Heroes Who Live On" are written for a younger audience, but make excellent material for "missions moments" in worship services, for use in Sunday School and Adult Bible Fellowship classes, and even for personal or family devotional times. Includes stories on the lives of Henry Holsinger, L.S. Bauman, Mary Bauman, R. Paul Miller, W.A. and Frances Ogden, Allen Bennett, Orville Jobson, Charles W. Mayes, Jake Kliever, Noel Gaiwaka, Ralph Colburn, and Evelyn Fuqua.

106 pages, paperback
ISBN #0884690830
$9.99 retail

Volume 1 also available for $6.99. Personalities include Alexander Mack, Florence Gribble, James Gribble, Estella Myers, Alva McClain, Russell Humberd, Homer Kent, Sr., Russell Barnard, Leo Polman, Harold and Ada Etling, Herman Hoyt, and Clyde Landrum.

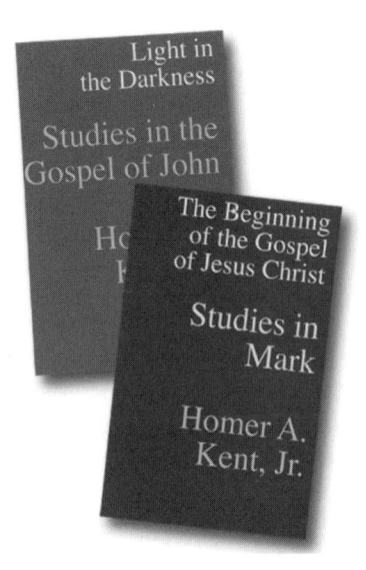

The Kent Collection

Dr. Homer Kent, Jr. taught for 50 years at Grace Theological Seminary and Grace College in Winona Lake, Indiana and was president for ten years. Widely respected as an authority on the New Testament and Greek, he has authored commentaries on 15 New Testament books. They are being updated and re-issued by BMH Books as The Kent Collection, beginning with *The Beginning of the Gospel of Jesus Christ: Studies in Mark*. Succeeding volumes include commentaries on the Gospel of John, the Epistle of James, and more. For a complete listing log onto www.bmhbooks.com.